THE WORLD IS
OUR CLOISTER

Winchester, UK
Washington, USA

First published by O Books, 2007
O Books is an imprint of John Hunt Publishing Ltd.,
The Bothy, Deershot Lodge, Park Lane, Ropley, Hants, SO24 0BE, UK
office1@o-books.net
www.o-books.net

Distribution in:

UK and Europe
Orca Book Services
orders@orcabookservices.co.uk
Tel: 01202 665432 Fax: 01202 666219 Int. code (44)

USA and Canada
NBN
custserv@nbnbooks.com
Tel: 1 800 462 6420 Fax: 1 800 338 4550

Australia and New Zealand
Brumby Books
sales@brumbybooks.com.au
Tel: 61 3 9761 5535 Fax: 61 3 9761 7095

Far East (offices in Singapore, Thailand, Hong Kong, Taiwan)
Pansing Distribution Pte Ltd
kemal@pansing.com
Tel: 65 6319 9939 Fax: 65 6462 5761

South Africa
Alternative Books
altbook@peterhyde.co.za
Tel: 021 447 5300 Fax: 021 447 1430

Text copyright Jennifer Kavanagh 2007

Design: Stuart Davies

ISBN-13: 978 1 84694 049 1

A CIP catalogue record for this book is available from the British Library.

Printed in the US by Maple Vail

THE WORLD IS OUR CLOISTER

A GUIDE TO THE
MODERN RELIGIOUS LIFE

JENNIFER KAVANAGH

BOOKS

Winchester, UK
Washington, USA

by the same author
Call of the Bell Bird

For my mother and father
who led the way

Sacramentality implies a real continuity between the everyday and the liturgical, between the body and the spirit, between earth and heaven.

Thomas Matus

CONTENTS

Acknowledgements vii

Chapter 1. Introduction 1
Chapter 2. A Life apart 12
Chapter 3. Out into the world 38
Chapter 4. In the world... 52
Chapter 5. ...but not of it 67
Chapter 6. Living in community 87
Chapter 7. Spiritual direction 99
Chapter 8. Spiritual practice 115
Chapter 9. Martha or Mary? 134
Chapter 10. Faith in action 149
Chapter 11. Obedience: faithfulness 164
Chapter 12. Poverty: simplicity 174
Chapter 13. Chastity 190
Chapter 14. Interspirituality 200

Taxing tasks 214
Follow-up questions 216
Further Reading 220

ACKNOWLEDGEMENTS

This book is about the lives of men and women who are trying to live their faith. It would not exist without the generosity of those who have shared their journeys. To all, profound thanks. Most have seen and approved what I have written; to any that I failed to contact, my apologies. I hope I have been true to what you wished to say.

The support of friends and family has been invaluable. I'd particularly like to thank Stephen Cox for the title and Lucinda Vardey for sharing her expertise on the monastic life, for pointing the way to O Books, and for her loving prayers.

All the references in the text are to the books and editions in Further Reading. Where there is more than one book by an author, the reference in the text gives the publication date.

JENNIFER KAVANAGH, 2007

1. INTRODUCTION

"Tell us," he said, "of a monasticism for our time, for the thousands who want it."

The speaker was an enquirer at a weekly outreach session in London, to which hundreds of men and women of all ages and backgrounds have flocked over the past five years, to share their spiritual paths and to find a spiritual home.

Those hundreds and thousands are no longer flocking to traditional forms of monasticism. Contrary to popular opinion, it is not behind monastery walls that most contemporary contemplative life is undertaken. There have always been those within the monastic tradition who are engaged in the world to some degree, and these are the orders to which people in the modern era increasingly feel drawn. Even more, men and women of different faiths feel called not to withdraw, but to live among others and actively engage with them: to live a committed life in the world. This book is an exploration of what it means to live as a contemplative in the world; it attempts to examine how people face the difficulties of being in the world but not of it – and what that means.

Such a life may not even be within the confines of a traditional religious structure. The religious landscape of the West is changing. In the States the growth of politically influential evangelical and fundamentalist churches has left behind a sharply declining religious liberalism. In the UK, despite changes wrought by immigration, attendance at churches other than Pentecostalist have shrunk by about 25% over the last seven years. Although the practice of other faiths has been on the increase, in 2000 just 7.9%

of the whole population in the UK were estimated* to have attended a church.

On the other hand, some 70% in the UK say that they believe in God and 50% believe in heaven. A surprising number of people of all faiths still recognise some notion of a religious identity and sign up to it when called upon to do so, as shown by hospital forms and returns from the UK census. And, over the past thirty years, the spectacular rise in numbers of people in the West seeking some kind of expression of their spiritual life has been well documented.

Drawing from stories of men and women across religious boundaries, this book affirms a way of life to which Christian, Buddhist, Hindu, Muslim and those with no label can relate. Transcending barriers of belief and practice, it offers guidance on how to practise the Perennial Philosophy, or the presence of God in our lives. For to have faith is not the same as having religion, and includes many who do not consider themselves part of any particular organised group and those who do not attend communal worship. The Catholic writer, Ronald Rolheiser, pithily refers to those who want church not faith and those who want faith not church. From the figures it would seem that the latter outnumber the former.

To have faith is to have trust: trust in a being, a power, a process both beyond us, and intimately within, something that is unknow-able, undefinable; faith would not be necessary if all could be known. Unknowing, we trust. Faith is all-encompassing: it is no more possible to have a little faith than to be a little bit pregnant; you either are or you are not; you either have faith or you do not.

---

* Peter Brierly, quoted in *The Friend*, 27 May 2005

This is not to claim any certainty or to rule out doubt. Learning is life-long; for many the seeking will be too.

I myself belong to the liberal unprogrammed Quaker tradition. Those I have interviewed include other Quakers, Christians of various denominations, Hindus, yogis, Buddhists, a Jain, a Sufi, Kabbalists, a devotee of Hare Krishna, as well as many without labels, both the unchurched and those who consider they have gone beyond the confines of one religion. All would say that they are on a spiritual path, that their faith influences the way they live, and that they have committed their lives to an expression of that faith. Most share an understanding of the commonality of faiths.

Many have faith; fewer live their faith. This book looks at some of those who try to do so and who consider that they have committed their lives to God. Although it examines briefly the monastic tradition and the priesthood, the emphasis is on those who live in the world without externally imposed discipline; who find their own way. It looks at how they do so, as solitaries or in community, as part of a recognised religion or not. It will also examine the relation between the interior life and its external manifestations, and considers how people find a balance between contemplation and engagement in their individual ways.

The World is our Cloister is not a book about theology. It is a book about experience: my own and those of other people of different faiths who are trying to live committed lives; the dozens of people I have interviewed, and those who have felt able to express their experience in their writings. I have spoken to those who have been ordained, those who have entered a monastic community – who have left it or stayed – as well as those who answer the call to live an active, engaged life in the world, and how

As a young child, I had many past life memories, and I remember talking to spirits or angels when I was very little. It wasn't odd in my family to have psychic abilities. My grandmother was an extremely gifted psychic, and both my mother and father listened faithfully to the "little voice within" who often guided them. So I was taught from my arrival to trust my intuition over all.

My mother was Catholic, and my father was Protestant. I was baptised and raised Catholic and went to Catholic school for nine years. I loved the church with a deep passion when I was a child. One of my fondest memories was of my first holy communion. After I had taken my first communion, I had to walk across the altar to return to my pew. As I passed the statue of the Blessed Mother, she smiled at me. It was a moment I was never to forget. Mary was my rock as a child. I'm not sure if it was that smile on my first Holy Communion day, or if it was something else. But it was always She to whom I prayed as a little one.

Daria wanted to be a priest, but realised that would not be given to her as a woman, though in adulthood her vocation is being realised, both in Christianity and in Vedanta.

Michael says, "I have always been aware of a God-shaped hole"; Jim talks of being "secure in God" at the age of six; Mirabai remembers dreaming of exchanging light from the third eye, but only if the eye of both people was open; Gill kept a spiritual diary from the age of 10 and at 11 knew she wanted to be a missionary. Warren, who says he had a typical Anglo-Jewish childhood, remembers thinking as a child: "I can't be the Messiah because I steal currants from the larder". Although not always recognised, the mindset, or rather the heartset, was in place early.

Such awareness does not always continue. For some the process is an ongoing growth; for others, like myself, there is a long period not so much of doubt as of lack of interest, years of what one man described as "a fog". Lives are taken up in building careers, families, nesting. The rest lies hidden. I once spoke of having lost my faith at the age of 18; someone gently rebuked me – "It went underground, that's all." Certainly in the period underground it was transformed; the new faith is of a more mature, conscious kind, a faith of wonder at the gifts of grace. The self that emerged was new and fragile; for months I felt as if I were treading on eggshells, not wanting to talk to anyone, not wanting my social self to trample on these shoots of growth.

A return to faith, or the beginnings of one, can be spurred in many ways: the result of suffering, trauma that cracks open the shell of self-protection, revealing a tender core blinking at the sunlight. Or a mystic experience, or a gradual sense that there must be more to life than this. The call, like the individual, will be unique. The experience of finding a spiritual home, however, is almost invariably described as an experience of quiet certainty: a "coming home" (even when, as in my case, there was no known past experience in that "home"). A Hare Krishna devotee described his faith as uncannily familiar; a Catholic nun felt like "a billiard ball falling into a pocket". Rather than finding a new path, we are recognising something that has been there all along. In being open to grace, true to our soul's purpose, we have been shown the jigsaw into which we fit.

But a call to what? The word "God" is a difficult one for many the way of devotion.

Initially my interviews included the question: "Are you happy with the balance of contemplation and action in your life?" The answer was almost invariably: "What's the difference?" It was a refreshing response: in general people seem to feel that action and contemplation are mutually exclusive, usually with the implication that somehow if you are engaged in the world, you are not very "spiritual" or if you lead an interior, prayerful life, you are not "doing your bit".

All of life is action, of course, and living a life for God will transform the way we live our lives. But it became clear that those who had a largely contemplative life – in an enclosed order or as a solitary in the world – would express their view of contemplation itself as action, whereas those more engaged with the world, whether politically or in terms of social action, described action itself as contemplation. Later on, we will explore the terrain between these two axes.

However one defines the differences, in each life, according to individual temperament, the balance of contemplation and engagement in the world will vary. This spectrum of spiritual expression is exemplified by the people in this book; their lives demonstrate the richness of possibility inherent in lives devoted to God.

Living in the world without the structures and material security of a monastic community, and in many cases without the support of a particular religious community, is not an easy option. The second part of the book considers how people live a sacramental life: how they juggle the demands of family and job on the one hand and their devotional life on the other; what helps them, what disciplines they find for themselves, and in what ways they need to distance themselves from the cultural norms of the society in which they live.

Christian monks and nuns of the past and the present day, such separation is a continuing form of expression of the God-filled life. Monks, attached to communities; hermits, living apart but in the main also with an attachment to a monastic community; friars whose calling is not one of communal stability but of a detached independence – all feel called to live apart from "the world". From the beginning a certain austerity and usually celibacy were built into an obedient way of life, with a regular pattern of communal and private worship. Work in the wider community or acts of charity have been prominent in some traditions, less so in more enclosed orders where the main emphasis has been on contemplation and self-awareness.

Josephus, the Roman chronicler of the Jews, writes that the oldest of the ascetics were the Essenes, pre-Christian Jews who lived a cenobic life in Palestine and Syria. About four thousand in number, they were devoted to study, prayer and acts of benevolence, and supported themselves communally by manual labour, especially agriculture. Some approved of conjugal intercourse; others abstained from marriage. They adopted children, accepted older proselytes and condemned slavery. They despised pleasure and luxury, wore simple white garments, ate a single dish and worked till sundown. Their novitiate was for three years. They prayed before sunrise and a priest said grace before meals. Strict obedience to their leaders was observed, with individual action permitted only in acts of mercy.

At the beginning of Christian monasticism men and women abstained from marriage and alcohol and were devoted to prayer, religious exercises and works of charity. The first religious order was formed in Southern Egypt by Pachomius, and by about 410 there were about 7000 monks, holding prayers and meals in common and leading a fully regulated life with work considered important for its own sake not just as an occupation. St Benedict, who lived in the early sixth century, established the roots of a monastic life that continues to this day. He introduced vows of obedience and stability, demanding a life-long commitment to a particular monastery. The vow of "conversion of manners" was a commitment of life in the monastery as a journey towards God. The monastic day was divided up into *opus Dei* (liturgy), *lectio divina* (spiritual reading), and *labor manuum* (manual work). By the early Middle Ages the Benedictine way had become the principal way of monastic life.

The influence of Benedict has reached beyond the confines of the monastic life, his "Rule" being a central part of not only Benedictine monasteries, but used by others, in and out of the cloister, as a rule for communal living. After the showing of "The Monastery" series in the UK, there was a rush on bookshops to buy "The Rule" and, caught by surprise, many shops sold out.

It is possible that there were organised monastic communities of women – the "veiled virgins" before those for men. In the early Middle Ages the sisters of the main founders of monasteries – Pachomius, Basil and Benedict – founded communities for women. In the early days nuns could leave the enclosures; in the Middle Ages the rule became stricter, more confined, and to this day there are more enclosed orders for women than for men. The rule of the Poor Clares (the second order of St Francis) is one of great poverty, seclusion and austerity.

The Carmelites, an order which included St Thérèse of Lisieux and St John of the Cross, originated in the twelfth century as a group of hermits living on Mount Carmel. They were not monks but lay people living as solitaries in a loosely connected group. Our Lady was the source of the interior spirit of Carmel: the perfection of the Carmelite ideal. In the late sixteenth century St Teresa of Avila gave a new impetus to the Carmelite way of life, combining the silence and solitude with community living, and adding the specific mission of praying for the Church and the whole world. They were given their Rule by St Albert of Jerusalem: "Let each remain in his cell or near it, meditating day and night on the Law of the Lord, and vigilant in prayer, unless he is legitimately occupied in something else." It was to be "a contemplative apostolate to other potential apostolates... a school of prophets" (Merton, 1976: 92).

In the early thirteenth century, partly in reaction to what they saw as too much power in the Benedictine model, there sprang up a movement of mendicant friars, notably the Dominicans and the Franciscans, a broad order devoted to poverty. On the death of St Francis, squabbles arose about issues that still face us today. The purists said that they should "own nothing", others emphasised that they lived in the world.

The later Middle Ages was the heyday of monasticism in the West. From that era come the great abbeys of the Benedictines and the Cistercians. New orders called Clerks Regular came into being, religious institutes of men, combining an emphasis on a particular kind of work, such as education, retreats or the preaching of missions with the solemn vows and common life of monks, though without the obligation of choir service. Clerks Regular are, unlike monks, primarily devoted to the sacred ministry and, because of their occupations, are less given to the monastic practice of austerity. The best known of these are the Jesuits, an order devoted to education, which was founded in 1540. Another group that comes under this heading are the Salesians, an active apostolic order founded in 1859 by Don Bosco, "the priest of street children". His mission was clear and simple: to be a friend to children who were poor, abandoned, or at risk – and, in so doing, to be a friend to Christ. There are now over 40,000 Salesian priests, brothers, sisters, and lay people working in 120 countries.

Josh, an Indian Salesian in his thirties, is based in Rome, on loan from his missionary province in India, living and working at the Salesian university. He wears casual clothes, only dressing in a cassock for services, when the congregation expects it.

Josh found his path at an early age. When he was 15, he wrote, without the knowledge of his parents, for details of the Don Bosco summer camp – and, finding Don Bosco a role model, became clear about his own path. He attended a college in Kerala which felt like a community, so it felt natural to go on to the novitiate. He took his final vows in 1992 and was sent to Rome.

In being true to his whole self, the absorption of his Indian identity has been an important theme in Josh's spiritual life. His Master's thesis was on Abhishiktananda, the Frenchman who co-founded the first Christian ashram in India and, just before taking his final vows, Josh felt a need to be enriched by Indian spirituality. He undertook a course of Vipassana meditation, and has continued to do so every year. The personal practice which sustains him at times of trouble is a combination of prayer and meditation. Sitting on the floor of the chapel looking at the crucifix gives him depth and constancy.

After some doubts about his worthiness, his ordination as a priest in 1996 was the moment he had been waiting for. Josh sees the nature of the order as contemplation in action, himself as a priest "with and for the people", though his career so far has been in the academic world. I asked if he didn't feel disappointed about not following his role model into work with street children. He did not answer directly, but said that in 2001, after spending four years back in India, there had been a tussle for him between Rome and India. His obedience teaches him that you can do good wherever you are. While in India, he met Mother Teresa, a spiritual guide for the Salesians, and wondered what was so special about this little woman. It was an important moment, he said, to realise that "God will choose the simple as his instruments".

Modern monasticism

So what of life in a modern monastery or convent? Even after the Second World War, monastic life, particularly for the novitiate, was austere: "We were under a rule of silence for all but two hours a day; and forbidden to talk to women, lay people and all members of the community except, in theory, the Abbot, and very much in practice, the novice master" (Boulding, 143). In some monasteries, novices were kept apart from the main community and not allowed home for four years. Living conditions too were spartan: "[We] spread an old blanket on the floor and make our ablutions in an old tin bath or wash-bowl" (Boulding, 116). Very different from the cells *en suite* of today!

The Second Vatican Council had a big impact on monastic communities, which were encouraged to be more open in their thinking, both in being more welcoming to those appearing on their doorstep and being more aware of and responsive to the real problems in the world. Many found the increased openness a problem. How to be aware of the world's problems and yet maintain an inner peace in which to listen to the whisperings of the Spirit?

Unlike the popular picture, monastic life today is not all solitude, prayer and the freedom to contemplate the ineffable mysteries of life. Different orders have always had their different characteristics, suitable for different kinds of calling. Some like the Poor Clares, remain enclosed, in for life, never to leave the walls or to see their families; others have concentrated on apostolic work: active service in the community. Daily work may be solely to support the community life of the convent – in building or growing vegetables; to support it financially by selling crafts and honey made by the community; or in the outside world as nurses, teachers, or in missionary activity at home or abroad.

The increased openness of monastic life has led to a loosening of some of the austerities of previous generations. In the Center of Renewal, a Franciscan convent near Niagara in the USA, elderly nuns remember with some nostalgia the more austere practices of their youth. Today, the sisters in practical mid-calf dresses and short veils watch television, run a car, shop and even take tea in the local village tea-shop. There is both loss and gain; one sister referred to the loss of "the commonality of the habit".

The habit in most orders is less all-enveloping and formal than it used to be, making concessions for what, for many, is a more active life. As early as the 1960s, the Trappist monk, Thomas Merton, had a policy of not wearing clerical dress "in the world". Today Aquinas and her sisters dress in a purple skirt and white "alone", monasticism is actually about community. There have, however, been many who have been drawn to a solitary quest for God. By the time Christian monasticism began, eremitism was already an established spiritual discipline in Eastern religions. To persevere in prayer and fasting, renouncing the desires and needs of the material world to achieve union with God and to purge and purify the body, mind and soul was considered one of the highest callings of Indian religious life. The image of the ascetic Hindu yogi is a cliché of the popular imagination. Skeletal, dressed only in a loin cloth, hair streaming down his back, he is the epitome of self-denial and contemplation. The *sannyasi*, too, is a familiar figure: an older man in single piece of saffron cloth, he has given up the world, carrying a bowl from village to village, begging for food, not money – he is not permitted to handle money. Hindu ascetics are independent individuals, following their individual paths, and quite separate from the life of temples and formal "religion".

Eremitism also formed an early and continuing thread in Christian religious life. St Antony, c 270, led a solitary life in a hut in the Egyptian desert for about thirty-five years until, asked for guidance by would-be disciples, a community of "Desert Fathers" arose around him. The Syrian monastic tradition both in its beginnings and today has been largely eremitical, and in the West the tenth and eleventh centuries saw a return to the eremitical way of life of the Desert Fathers. In modern times hermits are still highly regarded within the Church: Thomas Merton writes: "A Christian hermit can, by being alone, paradoxically live even closer to the heart of the Church than one who is in the midst of her apostolic activities" (1976: 58).

It is considered "good practice" for monks to spend years in community before being permitted to answer the call for life as a hermit. In the seventh century the Venerable Bede describes St Cuthbert's retirement to the solitude of Farne Island:

> So in that same monastery he fulfilled many years; and at last, with the goodwill of his abbot and brethren to company him, he set out in deep delight towards that secret solitude for which he had so long desired and sought and striven. The coming and going of the active life had done its long work upon him, and he rejoiced that now he had earned his right to climb to the quiet of meditation upon God.
>
> *Waddell*, 21

A description of a journey in the opposite direction gives a poignant picture of the joys of solitude:

> The old man…told them how "the sparseness of those who at that time dwelt in the desert was gracious to us as a caress; it lavished liberty upon us, in the far-flowing vastness of that solitude." But others came to know the sweetness of the quiet which their coming destroyed…Sublimity was gone: let him make up for it by obedience. So the old man came back from the desert, now a thoroughfare, to submit to the yoke of his abbot's will and the friction of living among men.
>
> *ibid.*, 19

The lives of a hermit and a monk can be combined. This elasticity of forms was present in early Christian and Eastern monasticism, and set an example for the Camaldolese, a Benedictine order formed in the eleventh century. Forms of life range from reclusion – whether temporary or permanent (in which the hermit simply lives within the confines of his cottage and garden) – to the regular hermitage life (a balance of solitude and community, with the daily divine office and Eucharist, etc., celebrated together) to the rural and urban monasteries, where the life is much more communal.

The mother house (founded by St. Romuald), with hermitage above and monastery below, is in the Tuscan mountains in Italy; other branches are to be found in a number of countries, including in the USA. The branch at Big Sur, California, urges contemplative prayer through solitude, silence and fasting. "We are a monastic and contemplative community, in the Benedictine tradition, with an emphasis on both solitude and community. This is a difficult balance, and requires specific human skills and a certain level of spiritual development."

The contribution of the separated life

Many of the apologists for the monastic life are actually arguing for the importance of a contemplative life, not necessarily for living apart: references to a person who has dedicated his or her life to seeking God can be applied to those living in the world too. When the French monk/swami, Abhishiktananda, says that "being is the most intense form of action", or that "no external movement in the physical world is so intense as the movement at the heart of the atom, through which indeed it exists. So it is with us; and that is our essential vocation as monks, nuns, contemplatives" (quoted in Stuart, 117), he speaks for us all. The implication that such a vocation is only for monks and nuns, and is only possible within a sequestered life, however, is, in my view, mistaken.. We may agree that "God dwells only where man steps back to give him room" (*ibid.*, 170), but stepping back is an interior movement, not necessarily a geographical one. It does not follow that a monastery is the only place where God can dwell.

Another justification of the contemplative life is often made on the grounds that prayer is active, "doing something", has "relevance". But to argue from such a "materialistic" perspective is to relinquish half the argument. So what is the point of living apart from the rest of humanity? The Buddha set a high value on the presence of monks and nuns in society. He considered the ordained *sangha* (community) fundamental to Buddhadharma (the attributes peculiar to Buddhas). He felt it crucial that there should be some who practise the *vinaya*, the Buddha's guidelines on conduct, to its fullest extent. The Dalai Lama "insists on detachment, on an unworldly life, yet sees it as a way to complete understanding of, and participation in, the problems of life and the world. But renunciation and detachment must come first" (Merton, 1973:113).

Several Buddhist monks and nuns have written about the increased focus of monastic living, the ability to clear the mind and concentrate on living the precepts. Without having to concentrate on making a living or supporting a family, and without being distracted by the activities and values and clamour of the external commercial world, there is more mental and spiritual energy to do interior work. The structure, silence and solitude of the prayerful life enable concentration on the quality of life, not its quantity. Thomas Merton sums it up this way:

It is true to say of every Christian that he is in the world but not of it. But in case he might be likely to forget this – or worse still in case he might never come to know it at all – there must be men who have completely renounced the world; men who are neither in the world nor of it. In our day, when "the world" is everywhere, even in the desert where it makes and proves its secret weapons, the solitary retains his unique and mysterious function...Withdrawal from other men can be a special form of love for them... The monk has all the more of a part to play in our world, because he has no proper place in it.

1976: 57, 58, 66

And Abhishiktananda says:

You, the monk, are here in the name of the church mystically to partake of the sacred waters of the source and thus to share with your brothers what you receive from their life-giving touch...You are the acosmic one, the one who stands fixed where all things have their beginning and ending.

(168-9)

Many of those who commit their lives to an order believe with Merton that "the monastery is the centre of the world", and that they are not so much escaping from the world as entering into the centre of it, and praying from there. Their commitment to God is on behalf of all humanity; their connectedness means that what they do with single-minded devotion is on behalf of all mankind, indeed, some argue, of all sentient beings. Whereas all belong to God, some live in the consciousness of it, and make a profession of that consciousness. The Benedictine Dame Maria Boulding writes that

> if it is true that we are all organically linked together within the life of Christ...then any fruitful activity by any member of Christ is done in the power of that life and belongs to us all...a dedicated life at the heart of this body thereby contributes in some unseen way to the vigour and fertility of the whole.
>
> (27)

Some stress the prophetic responsibility of those living a detached life. The identity and vocation of monks and nuns is seen as one of "people who have consciously and deliberately adopted a mode of life which is marginal with respect to the rest of society, seeking a certain distance from that society and a freedom from its domination and its imperatives, but nonetheless open to its needs and in dialogue with it" (Merton 1980: 218).

The element of sacrifice is very real for many Christians: taking monastic vows for the whole of life is to sacrifice all for God.

Vows

Gandhi had an interesting perspective on the subject of vows. He described a vow as more than a rule – more an existential pledge, a self-committal, and part of a preliminary discipline. Although in practice he was flexible – making exceptions for people living in poverty, for instance – he "began to attach special importance to the vow, not as a formalistic framework to keep one on the rails so to say, but as a way of entering more deeply into the truth, of being in the truth, of belonging to it, being rooted in it". His friend, Andrews, was against vows, saying that "life is always a growth into something new and unexpected and original" (Chatterjee, 69), and another friend described a vow as a crutch, and the vow-maker on the moral sphere not the spiritual. Even the Trappist Thomas Merton considered that a monastic life without vows is quite possible and perhaps desirable.

In Buddhism vows are considered to have such power that without them it is hard to progress. But the former Buddhist monk, Jack Kornfield, warns against too much rigidity:

> Even though teachers and communities may expect us to swear fealty, to take vows, to join for life, we do not need to take a permanent spiritual vow. Even permanent vows must be renewed. Yes, we must be patient and committed, but the true vow of the spirit is to honor our own integrity, awakening and compassion, no matter what changes in circumstances they call for.
>
> (242)

The Spirit is dynamic.

Problems

The ideal of monastic living is a magnet to many God-filled souls, and I have spoken to many who cast a yearning eye towards such a single-pointed existence without the responsibilities and distractions of life outside. A prayerful routine in a secure environment can be attractive, and some of the older people I interviewed talked of the possibility of going to a convent to end their years. "After all," said one, "life outside is not so different: I'm poor, I pray, I don't have sex, and it would be nice to be looked after in a congenial community." However, human beings are fallible, and accounts of monastic life are full of the same squabbles, tensions, difficulties of living one with another as arise in family life. "The intention", said a former monk wryly, "is not always properly realised," and for many living in a same-sex community is the hardest part of the religious life. For some, as we shall see in Chapter 13, it is celibacy that is most taxing,

Merton found even in a Trappist monastery that the silence was external and no mention was made of interior silence. Monks and nuns can be as busy and preoccupied with matters of administration and the work of the convent, as wedded to a sense of self given by their occupation, as anyone in the daily world outside. Dom Philip Jebb, headmaster of Downside school, talks of being overwhelmed with the work. Solitude can be hard to find. Perhaps the Buddhist orders that ask no work of monks after ordination organise things better.

The monastic life is no antidote to doubt. The struggles, the dry times, go on even for those most experienced in their vocation, and when you have given up all for God and there is little to distract you, the doubt can be more all-encompassing.

Validity

To identify a mystic life with a monastic one is a mistake. The Dutch Catholic priest, Henri Nouwen, says that "mysticism is the opposite of withdrawal from the world" (1995:177), and Evelyn Underhill illustrates the point with examples of mystics' creative activity in the world, including Paul, Teresa of Avila,

Augustine and Catherine of Siena. Although the explicit intent of the monastic experience is to commit oneself to God, and surely that must be to seek direct experience of God, mystics have not always been acceptable in a monastic, or indeed a church, context. In some cases mystics have been too individualist, too critical of social conventions and the establishment from which some of the monastic communities are drawn.

Meister Eckhart had to tread a careful path, and the mystic ends of most traditions have been branded as heretic: the fate of the Rosicrucians and Cathars bears witness to the prejudice against divergence from the structures and dogma of the Church. The Kabbalists and the Sufis have not always been accepted by the mainstream, and the Quakers were also persecuted, although more for their non-conformism than their religious practices. Although some of the most famous Christian mystics have come out of the monastic tradition – unlike Judaism and Islam, Christianity does not have a separate mystic branch – some of those too have been persecuted.

Roger Housden writes:

By the Renaissance, mystical experience had become not only suspect but verging on the unholy. With the rise of Protestantism, the Roman Church proclaimed it was necessary to "reconquer the world for Christ" with the result that outer action, rather than inner experience, came to be the dominant value of religious life....Protestantism did little to right the balance, stressing ethics and morality alongside social action.

(81)

The trend has continued. Many of those who have written about spiritual engagement in the world have had as their starting point an attack on the validity of monastic life. Such a view treats monastic or the "religious" life as irresponsible, an escape. In Gandhi's view, "Meditation, the life of contemplation as such, smacked of spiritual luxury, as much out of tune with reality as the palaces of marble and concrete that stand cheek by jowl alongside the hovels of the poor" (Chatterjee, 10). Even the mediaeval mystic, Meister Eckhart, has no time for withdrawal. Wisdom "is not to be learned by world-flight, running away from things, turning solitary and going apart from the world. Rather one must learn an inner solitude, wherever or with whomsoever he may be" (quoted in Sinetar).

The Tibetan Buddhist nun, Tenzin Palmo, holds the opposite view – that it is life in the world that is an escape. When we have a problem, we can call a friend, switch on the TV. A hermit has no one to turn to but herself. There is no escape: in solitude you have to face yourself.

But others in the religious life have questioned the validity of monasticism. What right do we have to concentrate on our souls and shut out the world? William Penn expresses an early Quaker view:

True godliness don't turn men out of the world but enables them to live better in it and excites their endeavours to mend it...Christians should keep the helm and guide the vessel to its port; not meanly steal out at the stern of the world and leave those that are in it without a pilot to be driven by the fury of evil times upon the rock or sand of ruin.

Quaker Faith & Practice, 23.02

At the time of the Vietnam war, Henri Nouwen stayed for seven months in a Trappist monastery, and wrote in his diary of feeling like a creature in Noah's Ark, "sitting on the top of a mountain while the world around me is washed away" (1995:113). He found

> a strong contrast between notes on the joy of God's presence, the silence and quietude of the monastery...the beauty of nature, and notes on hunger in Africa and India, torture in Chile, Brazil, Vietnam, wars everywhere, and the general state of misery of the world. It almost seems as if there were two persons in me experiencing life quite differently, praying differently, and listening differently. I started to wonder how they both could live together in peace.
>
> *ibid.,* 115

Writers such as Thomas Merton and Thich Nhat Hanh make it clear that finding self-awareness by necessary periods or a lifetime of withdrawal is only half the journey. The process is to make one more able to work for others; in Christian terms to build God's kingdom on earth.

> Only under certain circumstances is withdrawal from the world needed. Anchorites, who are nothing more than professional obsessives, have given the impression that the desert or mountains are the place where the mystic must spend his whole life. They have mistaken a thread for the whole carpet.
>
> *Shah,* paraphrasing Saadi, 99

In Eastern religions devotees are bid to work towards

self-realisation so that they will then be fit to bring their wisdom to bear on the suffering of the world. But how many achieve self-realisation? Does this mean that the millions working towards this end do not contribute to the world, but only to their own soul's development? "The man must not rest in this divine union. He must return to this world of unreality, and in the downward journey must keep the ordinary laws and creeds of man" (Florence Lederer quoted in Shah, 323).

Another criticism is of the rigid structures and outdated attitudes of Christian monasticism. Merton, writing in the 1960s, just after the Second Vatican Council, was critical of what he saw as hangovers from a mediaeval monasticism. Though he saw its strengths, he was concerned about its highly ritualised, aristocratic, even feudal character. He gives a trenchant warning against continuing with a system that needs reform: [Accepting that monasticism is essentially medieval] "takes for granted that 'the contemplative life' is sterile, foolish, wasteful, selfish and that it serves no purpose but to keep monks immature, walled off from contemporary reality, in a state of self-delusion, dedicated to childish formalities" (1980: 4). As we shall see in the next chapter, some vocations were damaged by such misconceptions about the reality of the religious life.

Certainly, in reading accounts of monastic life in that post-war generation in the British Benedictine tradition, the transition from public school to seminary and abbey seems to have been a smooth one. For many the problems arose later when a different kind of life and social stratum intruded. For some, I dare say, the intrusion never occurred. Even today, meeting some monks, one encounters a lack of awareness of "how the other half live", a naïvety about social conditions outside the privileged bastions of public school and seminary.

Such establishment life is a long way from the disciples' response to Christ's call to leave all and "follow me", and there is a danger that the institution can take precedence over the reality of vocation, and destroy the very purpose of the monastic life. As numbers dwindle, however, communities have felt marginalised, and there is evidence that in some cases they have embraced their status: still separated, not as a privileged class but as outsiders that can speak for others living on the margins of society. Closer, surely, to the way of life that Jesus asked for.

Active contemplation

The Salesian Josh may speak of his order as being "of the people and for the people" but his own role as a teacher of seminarians is a rarefied one. Mother Teresa's Missionaries of Charity, on the other hand, are the most commonly identified with the poorest and most marginalised in society, and move among them from a perspective in their own lives of the greatest simplicity. Nuns of the contemplative branch support their active sisters in prayer. The Little Brothers of Jesus, founded by Charles de Foucault, also strive to live and work alongside the poor. "The Little Brother may not have a life apart. He must choose a village, a slum, a nomadic town and live as all the others live, especially as the poorest live" (Carretto, 102). Their vocation is "contemplation in the streets", loving your neighbour as yourself. "The desert is a stage in the journey" (ibid., 74).

The standard of living of many hermits is also more on a level with that of the poor: the tramps and "gentlemen of the road". In

India *sannyasi* queue up together with the poorest of the poor for free meals doled out from religious and social service establishments.

In recent years there has been a growth of less orthodox, more ecumenical orders. The international community of Taizé in S.W. France has become a magnet for young people from all over the world to spend a few days or weeks in communal living, bible study, singing and regular prayer. Several thousand people gather throughout the year. The core group of resident brothers live from their work alone and visit the poorest places in the world to express solidarity and to listen. They wear no habits outside the liturgy – a welcome confusion of the sacred and the secular.

The Brothers and Sisters of Jerusalem are a contemplative order of nuns and monks with a new flexibility. Having lived in the Sahara desert for two years, a former Sorbonne Chaplain, Fr. Pierre-Marie Delfieux, felt called to find the "desert in the city" and the community was formed in the 1970s to create an oasis of prayer and peace in the modern desert of the city, an urban monasticism. Unlike most orders, it is expanding, with five centres in France, one in Brussels, and one in Canada. Like Taizé, the style is simple, with no chairs in the church – the congregation sits on the floor. The Brothers and Sisters neither live in community nor own homes, but rent apartments; they work part-time to support themselves, and gather three times a day for prayer: the Office and the Eucharist.

Their Rule, *A City not forsaken,* includes the following:

The city represents one of the privileged meeting-places between God and mankind. Dwelt in, sanctified, consoled, made joyful by the Lord. §128 Your whole monastic responsibility is to keep yourself from the world without cutting yourself off; to be part of it but not absorbed in it. §138

The emphasis is on work:

Delight and imitate your God by your work. The Father works, creating, judging and upholding the world. The Son works, he who became a carpenter and who sustains the universe by his word. The Spirit works, untiringly renewing our hearts and the face of the earth. §23 By working, you also show solidarity with the urban world and the mass of his workers, whether working or looking for work, whether happy at it or putting up with it. §25 Whatever you do, do it wholeheartedly as for the Lord. §29

Members of the Sufi Naqshbandi Order, formed in the twelfth century, devote themselves to the ideal of being solitaries while still living in the world. After a period of external seclusion, they reach a state in which "the Heavenly Realm becomes manifest", which leads to a state of internal seclusion. "The internal seclusion means seclusion among people. Therein the heart of the seeker must be present with his Lord and absent from the Creations while remaining physically present among them."

****

What comes out of accounts of monastic life is that the same human problems remain both within and without the wall of the cloister. The difficulties of living with our fellow human beings, the ache of loneliness and the yearning for understanding and closeness are common to all – as human beings, we tend to ask too much of each other. But the joys too may be much the same. One Benedictine monk wrote: "I want solitude, companionship, prayer, activity, relaxation and fun, care of souls, all at once and not at all, inextricably mixed together, pressed down and running over" (Boulding, 177). What an expression of the joy of the religious life, whether enclosed or out in the world.

The essential aim of the religious life, whether in or out of a monastery, is inner transformation. "The real sannyasi is simply fixed inside. This is his only function in society and the Church" (Stuart, 300).

Those of us in the world have a lot to learn from the discipline and single-pointedness of the monastic ideal. A balance of both ways of life has a lot to offer humankind. This may take the form of a period of withdrawal in preparation for action, or an attempt to live on both levels simultaneously. Some ways of finding this balance are considered in the next chapter.

3. OUT INTO THE WORLD

A number of those drawn to the monastic life find it is not for them and leave at various stages of their profession. Karen Armstrong was a nun for seven years before her health, mind and spirit drove her to leave. Two of the people I spoke to had also had to relinquish their vocation. Mark was an Anglican Franciscan monk for six years before mental health problems overwhelmed him, and he had to leave the order. Sarah started her postulancy at a Benedictine convent. She didn't want to teach but was drawn to a literary life, so aimed at an enclosed order at a Benedictine house in Worcester, a bookish convent with a printing press. From 1986 she spent all her holidays and every other weekend there and devoted herself to qualifying as a librarian. At the time of decision, the end of her course at Oxford, she was sent to a priest psychiatrist, who startled her by saying that she had unresolved issues with her sexuality.

The convent suggested that she take some time to think. Sarah visited a friend in a French Benedictine convent, and found her behind a grille, with no opportunity for outside work, and a bell every hour to remind her about prayer. She then visited the only English-speaking enclosed community of Dominicans. There were only seven nuns there, with a woman with a first-class degree working in the laundry. She found their lack of freedom of action, their being at the beck and call of men and in the end a male decision to close them down, very depressing.

After the visit to the psychiatrist, Sarah realised that there had been a shift in the convent's attitude to her, and felt driven to abandon her vocation. After her initial anger, and her difficulties with hierarchy and authority, she realised that she had had a "medieval concept" of convent life, believing it would give her space for intellectual work while others did the manual work. Now in her thirties, an attender at a Quaker Meeting, with a partner and two children, she still thinks she might enter in old age. "You can ignore a vocation but you can't kill it."

Temporary monasticism

Thomas Merton talks about a possible way forward for the monastic way of life in a core of permanently committed monks, with others coming for two to three years, or on retreat. He puts forward the possibility of admitting married people, non-Catholics, even non-believers.

The idea of temporary monasticism is not a new one. Sufis are expected to go through a period of training – long or short according to capacity – before being considered sufficiently balanced to be "in the world but not of it". In Zen Buddhism the communities, according to Alan Watts, are unlike monasteries in a Western sense, more like training schools from which students are free to depart at any time without censure. Some will stay monks for a lifetime; some will become secular priests; others will return to the lay life. Although Chinese Buddhist masters will normally be monks, they are generally supported by large numbers of advanced lay students.

Temporary vows have also been acceptable at earlier stages of Christianity. An interesting and long-lasting early experiment was that of the *beguines*, a movement of women which began in the swell of Western interest in mysticism in the twelfth century, and continued mainly in the Low countries, through vicissitudes of persecution and civil wars, until the French Revolution. Small groups of women ran their own democratic communities in houses called *beguinages*. They did not make perpetual vows of chastity, poverty and obedience, as classical monks and nuns did. Their promises were only temporal and poverty was not necessary: a *beguine* had her own possessions and her own income. She promised celibacy and obedience but only as long as she remained in the *beguinage*. She was free to leave the convent at any moment, although on leaving she usually had to give up her rights to her house. Mechtild of Magdeburg, an unmarried laywoman who was a great influence on Meister Eckhart, was a *beguine* most of her life. A consistent critic of church corruption, she was driven from one town to another. She became a third order Dominican and in old age a nun.

In Tibetan Buddhism, alternating the householder and monastic modes of life is possible. Yvonne Rand, for instance, took the "Kitchen Sink Path" and writes, "I finally realised that what I am is a lay, ordained priest, a householder who practises periodically as a monastic" (in Mackenzie, 194). In the last century Abhishiktananda alternated his residence for many years between Santivanam, the Christian ashram he had started in Tamil Nadu, and a cave in the Himalayas. Such a practice was recommended too to Thomas Merton by some Tibetan rinpoches who warned him against absolute solitude.

Today, in Canada, Lucinda, a Roman Catholic who has also embraced the *bhakti* yogic path, is experimenting with a life that alternates being active in the world and a more contemplative existence. She and her husband, who trained as a theologian, are piloting a married monastic life, taking it in turns to alternate weeks "out", dealing with the bills and the demands of an external existence in the world, and weeks concentrating within.

The priesthood

I... am the priest, the yeast mixed into the masses of the world to make them rise and become the Eucharistic dough. I am the cosmic one; I belong to those whom the Lord sends right into the world to prepare his ways, consecrate the earth to him, and to bring in the Kingdom.

Abhishiktananda, 170

Monks, nuns and hermits are not the only groups whose role and identity sets them apart from the world. The priesthood too has been a powerful stratum of society, in the world but separated from it by its role and status. From Babylon to Ancient Egypt, only particular individuals were permitted to perform sacrifices and other rituals on behalf of the people. In latter-day Judaism too priests were the only ones permitted to approach the most holy items without profanity. Today, in the Japanese Soto Buddhist school the training and ordination is for the purpose not of monkhood but the priesthood.

However, not every religion makes a separation between monks and priests on the one hand and the rest of the population on the other. In Islam, for instance, the imam may have a full-time job in a large congregation, or a shared responsibility in a smaller one, but officially anyone can lead Islamic prayer. One imam said, "I'm not ordained. I don't have power. A Muslim is independent and answerable to God." A Jewish rabbi is not ordained either: he is a teacher rather than a priest. Pagan priestesses and priests are trained to conduct ceremonies, but are voluntary and unpaid with no specific position in the community.

In Hinduism priests lead a family life, often living in temples. They perform rituals such as birth and death ceremonies, fund raising, daily and festival worships. They are typically (but not necessarily) Brahmins and may have inherited the profession. Not all Brahmins have to be priests – in fact, these days they can be found in many walks of life, including charitable work with untouchables. *Puja*, worship which is often done in the privacy of a Hindu's own home, does not necessarily involve a priest. The priesthood is a large and multi-layered profession that does not have to be celibate, nor does it exercise any pastoral or social role.

It is in most denominations of Christianity that a priest's role is central. Only a priest may give the Eucharist and other sacraments; other duties include conducting services and taking pastoral responsibility for the parish. Speaking of the privilege of administering the Eucharist, one priest said, "I remember feeling a sort of helpless gratitude of being a steward of God's mysteries."

The role of a priest is to mediate between God and the people. That necessarily means an engagement with the rest of the world, and normally to live in it, although many Christian monks too are priests, and will in some cases live within the monastic community. The connection between monk and priest is not necessarily a happy one, but in some monastic communities it is taken for granted that men will be both. It does give the freedom of priestly life, and sometimes the pleasure of living with a small group instead of in a big institution.

Priests of Anglican and other Protestant denominations may marry, and increasingly allow the ordination of women; in Roman

Catholicism ordination is for celibate men only. In France, where Catholic priests are less part of the community than in England, there is a shortage of priests. As celibates, it is less lonely to live in a monastic community than out in the world.

Priests are of course separated by their vows, and often by their dress, although increasingly priests in some Christian denominations wear a cassock only for liturgical functions. The black habit is worn by ministers of the Orthodox Church and often by Roman Catholics; decreasingly elsewhere. The extent to which priests are engaged in social action varies a good deal too, and will often depend on the character of the congregation as well as of the priest himself.

It is noticeable that of those living a committed life priests are among those who take least time for themselves. Peter is an overworked Anglican priest with four rural parishes; Charles, an Anglican priest in a busy London parish, nominally has one day off a week and goes on an occasional retreat, but his life is generally divided between his parish duties and the demands of his family and the school run. Terry, a prison chaplain, finds his quiet time only on the drive to work and an occasional walk over the fields. He is uncompromisingly in the world. When I asked if he had ever thought of becoming a monk, his answer was "Certainly not!" At theological college he was "world-affirming" when others were world-denying. He thinks of himself as a maverick: he does not call himself Reverend or wear a dog collar.

Peter doesn't wear a dog collar either. He met me off the train wearing beads, a leather waistcoat and hat, and with long hair and a cigarette in his mouth. After dropping out of school, he lived in squats for some years until he was ordained 10 years ago. He felt an insistent call to priesthood, particularly in a rural setting. In answer to the question "What is your life's work?" he said, "To be true, to be myself."

He is writing a book about the meeting point of God and man: he feels the Church tries to align itself on that point and fails. Peter sees no distinction between contemplation and the active life: they are different ways of expressing love. "Brother Lawrence?* If we taught that in church, as we should, the church would die."

He considers himself in the world and of it; embracing the world. Inclusive.

Peter has written of his anger with the hierarchies and institutionalisation of the Church. "Where are the priests? Where are they? The priests of the alleys, the priests of the birds, the priests of the addicts, the priests of the alpha, the omega, the priests of the thin places?" (Owen Jones, 86). "Have we not taken God out of the world and put him, put her, into church, for our own practical convenience, done up Sundays in buttons" (*ibid.*, 129). "Church in its institutional sense is dying," he told me, "and a good job too."

"Why be a priest in it, then?"

"I need their rigidity, challenged by my fluidity."

Worker-priests

In 1989, while employed as a social worker, Hugh was ordained a priest in the Church of England. It was an unorthodox step, given that he was also a member of the Religious Society of Friends, and Quakers do not have a separate or paid ministry. "My disquiet

---

*The Practice of the Presence of God in all we do.

slipped away when I stumbled on the existence of what the church called non-stipendiary [unpaid] ministers (NSMs)." Hugh became what is called a worker-priest. He works full time but is at church three Sundays out of four and undertakes pastoral work. He wrote: "We assume the priesthood demands a particular social and professional setting (unhelpfully) as normative: stipend and housing from the church; assignment to a particular parish; an end to any previous work or employment, and some kind of elemental separation from others. Worker-priests or non-stipendiary ministers do not have that."

Hugh is an examining chaplain and has been the Bishop's advisor on child protection for many years. He believes in the Dominical sacraments (those given by Jesus – the Eucharist and baptism) and spends time with the dying. For him, death is not the end. He feels that being contemplative in the midst of work is what matters, not just in quietness. Jesus is important as the door, not the end.

Like Peter, Hugh has strong views about the paid clergy:

It is clear that…a great gulf remains between the world of work and the priest's calling as presently understood…We lack models of ordained men and women who manage effectively to discharge their duties as priests and who operate in a range of posts, jobs, roles and professions and who see these as being the places they pray, witness and celebrate the link between the transcendent and immanent.

The living out of the priest's office seems often to drift from the ontological and inspirational to the functional and tired. Of course there are exceptions, but many parish clergy drift towards becoming museum attendants: preserving the artefacts, discouraging innovation and preferring well-behaved visitors who admire the exhibits.

One answer to these criticisms, as Hugh found, was the movement of non-stipendiary ministers, or worker-priests. Worker-priests began as a missionary experiment in France and Belgium after the Second World War, seeking to reach the working classes, who had largely become alienated from the church. The worker-priests set aside their clerical garb and left their clerical dwellings to take jobs in factories and on construction sites, sharing the living and social conditions of local people.

Hugh writes on his website:

Some of the priests radicalised. Their consequent involvement in trades unionism and in the daily demands and compromises most working people face alarmed the hierarchy of the Roman church. It is claimed that the Vatican ordered the experiment to cease. Whatever the actual reasons, they were clothed in the assertion that paid "secular" employment was inconsistent with the calling and office of a priest.

Nonetheless, the French experiment was a factor that influenced the Second Vatican Council in its move towards increased openness in the Roman Catholic Church.

In the Church of England regulations were changed in the 1960s to allow men (it was only men at that time) to be ordained priest and continue in "secular" employment. It would seem that the main driver was not theological but practical – there were insufficient priests to support all the parishes. So the "normative" model of priesthood (stipend, parish, separation) was maintained and there was no explicit theological assertion that it might be right for a number of working men and women from all professions and jobs to be ordained.

Since then the Church of England has ordained many NSMs like Hugh, and like Terry too, who before becoming a chaplain worked as an NSM while running his own business. Abhishiktananda expressed his admiration of a particular worker-priest:

Monastic life, either alone or in community, runs such a risk of becoming commonplace...not to mention our self-satisfaction in our vocation. So when you see people slaving away like him, and constantly in touch with a pleasure-seeking and corrupted world...who even so preserve such a depth in their life, you rejoice in the world, and also have to make a humble self-examination.

Stuart, 156

Hugh feels that they provide an immeasurable additional resource but that the majority of dioceses do nothing to provide specialised support to them and appear to treat them as "assistant" clergy. Charles's view is not so positive. He feels the contribution of NSMs depends on their motivation. Some, he says, swan around on a Sunday and are not seen for the rest of the week. But the presence of, for instance, a retired person with a lifetime's experience can, he feels, be immensely valuable.

It could be said that if a special group of people, be they monks or priests, take the responsibility for spiritual life on themselves, it absolves others of that responsibility and disempowers them. Quaker practice goes beyond that of worker-priests. With no paid *or separated* ministry, they believe in "the priesthood of all believers". It is not the priesthood that has been dispensed with but the laity. All take responsibility for God's work and for the spiritual and pastoral roles of the priesthood.

Lay

The choice is not to be in the world or out of it. Over the centuries, different traditions have developed a variety of ways of service. From the beginning of monasticism there have been concessions for those who, for one reason or another, do not feel able to commit to total separation from the world. Lay brothers, for instance, are freed from duties at religious services and studies but perform manual labour and are bound by vows of obedience. Examples are Brother Lawrence in seventeenth-century France and the writer Wayne Teasdale in twentieth-century America.

The Third Order of St Francis (tertiaries) was established in 1221 and spread rapidly. These groups of lay people in association with the mendicant orders took part in all the religious exercises and good works of the community to which they were affiliated, but were not called upon to follow any rule of life. Originally St Francis did not intend to found an order, but when it became necessary, he had to provide for the mass of married men and women who were unable to leave the world or abandon their avocations. So, after the First Order (Franciscan monks) and

Second Order (Sisters of the Poor Clares) came the Third Order. "Regular" tertiaries formed themselves into communities and followed a religious life based on the rule of the third order; others, "secular", lived in the world. Soon other orders formed their own third orders, with Rules for ordinary people who wanted to serve God in their homes and communities. Examples of tertiaries include St Catherine of Siena and Angela of Foligno, and continue to this day.

Giles, a Franciscan tertiary since 1978, belongs to such a community, with separate governance from the linked first and second orders. They have a self-administered nine-fold Rule of life: Eucharist, prayer, retreat, study, self-examination (it used to be confession), work, simplicity, self denial (or self discipline) and obedience. Giles feels that he is a bit free and easy about parts of the tertiary Rule. The local church is broad and accepting. He co-leads a course on spirituality in a local adult education centre – helping people discover their own journey. An omega rather than alpha course, he said. He is writing a book about non-belief, going beyond belief, limitlessness.

The secular cleric makes no profession and follows no religious rule; he possesses his own property like laymen, he owes to his bishop canonical obedience, not the renunciation of his own will, which results from the religious vow of obedience; only the practice of celibacy in Holy Orders is identical with the vow of chastity of the religious. Such associations exist in a number of countries and on all continents.

Peter J is a lay member and trustee of the Amida Trust, an international *sangha* of socially engaged Buddhists of the Amida order. Called "a monastery without walls", the order uses the eight-fold Buddhist way "to discover and deepen Buddhist faith and put it into practice for the benefit of all sentient beings". The most simple and difficult aspect of Amidism, says their website, is to trust that one is acceptable just as one is. There is nothing to achieve, but there is a deep dynamic already at work in our lives and if we allow it then we will find ourselves seized by it. Amidism is a matter of awakening to this inner dynamic.

The structure provides for different ways of life: for *Amitaryas* who follow a rule of 42 precepts and live full-time religious lives, novices, ordained ministers and chaplains living in society, and lay members like Peter, who have made a serious commitment to the Buddhist path and taken up significant roles within the *sangha*. For Peter it is important that the order is active in the world, and that the set of precepts has been extended to include the wellbeing of the earth and its resources. Peter feels that, as a Pure Land path of Buddhism, the order echoes Quakerism in its emphasis on the need for the assistance of the Eternal Buddha (or the Spirit) rather than on achieving personal enlightenment by one's own efforts.

The Brahma Kumaris (daughters of Brahma) is an organisation which has always been run by women. It now has 5000 branches in over 80 countries and presents itself as a world-wide spiritual university. Its basic teaching is *Raja* yoga, a form of yoga that is expressed in meditation and a way of life in which the self is surrendered to God. The aims are soul-consciousness and purity; the practice ascetic. There is a growing emphasis on social and environmental action, education and human rights. The movement is also moving into management training, offering courses on positive thinking, stress reduction and leadership, with an emphasis on the importance of spirituality in business. The qualities it stands for are simplicity, responsibility, happiness, humility, honesty, respect, peace, love, tolerance, co-operation and freedom.

As we have seen, the choices facing those wishing to live a committed life are many and varied, from the enclosed monastic to a lay commitment. We now turn to those whose call is to live an engaged life in the world.

4. IN THE WORLD

Those who have renounced the world are the "known" yogis: all recognise them…But the hidden yogis live in the world. They are not known.

Sri Ramakrishna

Warren, now 72, is from a Rabbinic family. He had the "normal Anglo-Jewish upbringing". He was always more interested in the mysterious parts of existence than in its outward manifestation. After art school, he worked as a theatre designer then turned to writing, realising that philosophy and allied subjects were his metier. At about 30 he joined the Ouspensky school. For the first time he had found something purely esoteric. He stayed with them for some years, then moved to the Study Society, which he felt was closer to the teachings of Ouspensky. He then met someone who explained the principles of Kabbalah, and realised that was for him.

Warren's first book on the Kabbalah was The Tree of Life. *He has now written 16 books, and has been running an esoteric group for about thirty years. There are also groups in other countries, and people come to see him from all over the world. He has found no conflict between Ouspensky, the Kabbalah and cosmology. The more you teach, he says, the more you learn. Warren's origin is from the tribe of Levi: they were teachers, not priests. Their role is to bring "light unto the nations". When asked if he feels the balance of his life is right, his response is: "How can I complain?" He enjoys his teaching, has a wife twenty years younger than himself and, in a Jewish gesture, says: "I even make a living!"*

Warren's view of the role of religion is to bring wisdom down to earth. There are, he says, four journeys: we are incarnated to learn; we ascend to absorb philosophy and spirituality; we reincarnate to help, teach; we return up at the end of time. He feels that life is to be lived, meant to be enjoyed and developed.

Warren's study wall is full of esoteric symbols, mandalas, a celebration of the whole of existence: Jacob's ladder, a menorah, a Buddha, life, death, the heavens, the earth, and a luminous cosmological map on the ceiling, the Tree of Life, the Burning Bush, angels, male/female; the forms of life: mineral /vegetable/ animal/ human. There is even space for fairies in the garden. It is a collection of a lifetime – this room has travelled with him through life. Downstairs the meeting room is also full: he calls it "a temple". There is a plaster model of the historical Second Temple: the outer court which stands for nature; inner court for the soul; sanctuary for the spirit; Holy of Holies for the Divine.

Most people, by definition, live "in the world": it is from the majority that "the world" is made up. A tiny minority, as we have seen, have committed themselves for religious reasons to a life deliberately separated, geographically and culturally, from the rest. But it is wrong to imagine that it is only in those enclosures that people live committed lives. "The life of prayer, the life of contemplation, is simply to realise God's presence to us. It is therefore not a special way of life reserved for those few individuals who are called to get away from the world and to dwell in the deserts" (Abhishiktananda, 4). In this chapter we will look at the paths of some who have felt called to live their faith in the world. In the following chapters we will consider how they do so.

Non-monastic traditions

Although the monastic tradition is deeply rooted in some religious traditions such as Buddhism and Christianity, it is less important in others. Despite the example of the Essenes, monasticism has played no part in the history of Judaism. Even the Jewish mystics – the Kabbalists, the Hasidim - stay firmly in the world. The sacred book of the Hindus, the Bhagavad Gita, asks for detachment but not separation:

> The secret of action, says the Lord to Arjuna, lies in doing it as an offering to God, in the spirit of surrender to Him...The more a person is united with God, the less he is attached to the world...This however, does not mean withdrawal from the world and retirement to the seclusion of a hermitage in a forest...the Gita wants us to be actively engaged in the discharge of our duties but in a spirit of detachment... renunciation of the fruit of action but not of the act itself.
>
> *Suda*, 71

Islam has an ascetic tradition, but not a monastic one. Indeed the Koran explicitly states that Christianity created monasticism; Allah did not decree it (chapter 57) and it has no ordained clergy. The emphasis is on a Muslim's responsibilities in the world: no distinction is made between the sacred and the secular but on a way of life. Even in Sufism, its ascetic tradition,

> Systems that teach withdrawal from the world are regarded as unbalanced... The Sufi is an individual who believes that by practising alternate detachment and identification with life, he

becomes free. He is a mystic because he believes that he can become attuned to the purpose of all life. He is a practical man because he believes that this purpose must take place within normal society. And he must serve humanity because he is part of it.

Shah, 23

"The true saint [said Abu Sa'id] goes in and out amongst the people, and eats and sleeps with them and sells in the market, and marries, and takes part in social intercourse, and never forgets God for a single moment" (quoted in Spencer 319).

The Quaker way, too, is unequivocally in the world. Liberal Quakerism is by nature a mystic faith: the prime purpose in its meetings is a collective waiting upon God in stilling of the body and mind in order to be receptive to the Spirit. If a mystic experience is defined as an encounter with the Divine, the entire purpose of a Quaker Meeting for Worship is in preparation for that encounter. And, unusually (uniquely?) it is a mystic faith not restricted to any special group. It is open to all. As we have seen, there is no separated priesthood; all are equal before God and have an equal opportunity for access, an equal opportunity to become a channel for the Spirit, to "minister" – rise and speak what has been given.

But the Religious Society of Friends (to give it its formal name) is too a supremely practical faith. Instead of a creed, Quakers hold to testimonies as a guide to a way of life. Those generally acknowledged are: peace, equality, simplicity and truth, though others – such as a testimony to the earth – are often accepted and the divisions between them are somewhat artificial:

all is interconnected. There are no written forms to be signed up to; the exact interpretation will be according to individual conscience and experience. Most who come to Quakerism will find that these are already part of their private morality and a way of expressing the work of the Spirit in the world.

****

Whatever your yearnings, your work, your affections are, that is the place for your daily encounter with Christ. It is in the midst of the most material things of the earth that we must sanctify ourselves, serving God and all people. Heaven and earth seem to merge, my sons and daughters, on the horizon. But where they really meet is in your hearts, when you sanctify your everyday life.

Saint Josemaria Escriva

Saint Josemaria Escriva was the founder of Opus Dei, a branch of the Catholic church which encourages its members to live consistently with their faith, in the middle of the ordinary circumstances of their lives. The Second Vatican Council taught that all the baptised are called to follow Jesus Christ, by living according to the Gospel and making it known to others. The aim of Opus Dei is to contribute to that evangelising mission of the Church.

Bringing the religious life into the world in general makes us more open, more available. It is strange, then, that a movement such as Opus Dei should have brought upon it criticisms of secrecy, that in its "secularisation" it should seek to hide its existence in colleges, for instance, and so has been seen as an "infiltration" with proselytising intent, rather than a more egalitarian inclusion of the laity. "Secularisation" is not in any case a word I feel comfortable with. To me the sacred and the secular are one; in every act and being, the sacred *is* in the world, *is* the world.

Given what I had heard, it was good to meet Dani, a London member of Opus Dei, a very youthful 41. A "cradle Catholic", she was non-practising until the age of 13 when her Jewish mother was baptised. This had a powerful effect on Dani who started to question herself about the direction of her own faith. Soon afterwards she met a member of Opus Dei who persuaded her to come to a youth club which she loved. She joined the movement just before her 16th birthday.

It was, she said, "a love story. I've met God and I don't want to leave Him. Love is your driving force if you are committed." Dani has never felt called to the religious life, but has never wanted to be married either or to have children which she feels is also a vocation. Her own is apostolic celibacy, and to live her faith in the midst of the world. Since 1999 when she left college, where she studied catering and hospitality, she has lived and worked in an Opus Dei centre with other women, some of whom are not members. They live as a family rather than as a community, and have daily mass at the chapel in the centre. Dani is serene in the certainty of her faith, which was strengthened by a serious accident some 15 years ago when she and the other passengers in a minibus were unharmed after the vehicle turned over several times. She did not panic or pray, just wondered, "Why am I still here?"

She feels she is both Martha and Mary, and that she has a

good balance in her life. She moves jobs and accommodation as necessary for her calling. Dani is not lonely, but would be, she says, if she stopped praying. She has close friends, some of whom understand, and some who do not.

Opting out

Even in faiths that do have a monastic tradition, most people will opt to live "in the world". Those who try to live according to their faith will have chosen to be in the world while retaining some separation in terms of values and way of life. "Have chosen", however, is only a partial truth. Most will say that they feel called to a particular path by something beyond their own will.

The call to be in the world is not an easy one for everyone. It has surprised me how many of the people I have interviewed have either now or in the past had hankerings for the monastic life. Mike talks of his struggle between being in the world and wanting to join the Franciscans, though he wasn't happy with their theology. Although absorbed in the work he was doing, "I didn't feel part of the world's ways." He was working with disturbed kids, giving him hell. He had asked for "'the toughest job you've got. I've got other resources to draw on.' I had to take their worst. When they had given their worst and I still returned them love was the only point at which a healing occurred."

He can still remember the moment of deciding to join the Franciscans, then a few moments afterwards fell in love with his future wife. "I had to make that decision in order to be released from it. It was guidance. I had something else to do." He wanted to become more devotional, but had useful things to do on the outside.

In the last chapter we read of Hugh, a Quaker who felt called to be ordained. Farley's journey has taken the opposite direction. Ordained a priest in the Episcopal Church in the USA, he turned to teaching as a more rewarding activity. After some years of teaching and officiating at the occasional service, he felt his spiritual life to be unsatisfying. When his mother died, Farley realised that her inherited Quakerism was an element in her that he admired, and in his 50s he started to attend Quaker meetings. He joined the Religious Society of Friends while maintaining his licence as a non-stipendiary minister. Like Hugh, he has managed to keep the two allegiances, although his primary home is with the Quakers, and in the world.

Wendy, a poet living in London, was admitted into the Catholic Church in her sixties, and received instruction from the Jesuits with the intention of entering the Dominican order as a postulant. A few weeks before she was due to enter, having taken leave of her family, she "changed her mind". Asked why she decided not to enter, Wendy said that it was not a decision, it simply became clear that she needed to be with her family. Wendy now lives as a lay person close to the priory, attending Mass daily and serving the local community as well as spending time with her daughters and grandchildren. "Family life", she said, "is part of the incarnation."

Without Labels

To define even recognised faiths and philosophies by labels is to distort. In writing a book like this it is almost impossible not to use generally accepted and convenient pigeonholes, but a practitioner of Tibetan Buddhism told me that in Tibet they do not use the word "Buddhist": that is a term for the convenience of Westerners.

Similarly the word "Hindu" means a person who lives beyond the Indus river, and was cultivated mainly by Swami Vivekananda in the 1890s when he attended an international conference of world religions in Chicago. "Christian", "Jew" and "Muslim" may more accurately describe the beliefs of those so described, but in each case there is considerable variation according to different denominations, and individual belief may be more complex still.

Not everyone feels the need, or indeed feels able, to constrain their faith within a traditional framework. A recent global interfaith survey, run by The International Interfaith Centre and covering 335 respondents in 40 countries, revealed an interesting array of self-descriptions under the heading of "religion/spirituality". Apart from those belonging to the usual religious denominations, others attempted to define their paths by refining traditional labels such as: Liberal Christian, Celtic Christian, Progressive Christian or Reformed Christian; or combining them: Christian Buddhist, Christian and Mystic, Half Christian, half-Muslim, Christian practising Zen Buddhist meditation or Pagan and shamanism. Wider descriptions included: "Universal Spirituality", "All", "Interfaith" (from several, including an Israeli rabbi), "Religion of Love", "Practiser of several religions and philosophy", "Religious – no church", "Non-denominational" and "My own".

Another survey carried out in the USA in the early 1980s for a book on voluntary simplicity found that whereas 88% said that they followed an "inner growth" practice, and 55% said they practised meditation, only 20% identified themselves as part of a traditional religion. Comments like "I'm always aware of the Spirit" and "I like to sit alone on a rock and just open my mind up to everything...And I do believe in God" were common among those who declined a label (Elgin, 62). As researchers at Lancaster University have found (quoted in *The Friend*, 27 May 2005), "people increasingly engage with the sacred in ways that are unrelated to the church and to formal religion".

The Retreat Association says on its website that increasingly it is providing resources for those inquirers who are seeking to further their spiritual journey but are not part of the established church. These people are sometimes on the edges of the church because they feel hurt, disillusioned or no longer nourished by it. Others have never been a part of a church and have no desire to be. There can be isolation in the spiritual life. Many, courageously faithful to their own inner voice, rejecting religious certitudes that are not for them, are unaware that they are not alone. In isolation it is easy to believe that "religion" always comprises a set of dogmas, set devotional practices, imposing a communal identity on its followers. Even in traditional religion that is no longer always the case. As I have talked to Anglicans and Catholics, I find there is more diversity, more flexibility, than I understood when I was growing up. They too have changed, and the churches that some of us fled have more to offer us than we realise.

Ecumenical groups such as the Abbey community on Iona and the monastic community of Taizé in France have released many from the rigid dogma of their childhood, and have provided starting points for seekers to a path that reveals their authentic selves.

A former Anglican Franciscan monk and self-confessed mystic told me that he regards much New Age "mysticism" with scepticism, describing it as "angel card spirituality", and expressed the danger of "becoming this and that". Such accusations can fairly be aimed at some who dip in and out of a variety of schools of religion. Seeking for wisdom outside ourselves, in one master and the next, one holy book or another, shifting allegiance from one set of rules to another, will only prolong restless dissatisfaction. What I sense in the self-descriptions above, however, is not a superficial eclecticism but a struggle to be true, a recognition that one size does not fit all, that an inner voice is not expressed by any of the available labels. Jan, who has had many peak experiences and felt the spirituality of her being at a very young age, has struggled to find "a structure that holds my experience".

Seeking within will cause movement, but it will be a coherent movement of the heart in its organic growth and increased awareness. It is in answer to inner promptings that we may find a practice, a tradition, that answers our needs, for that time. We cannot say where it will lead us in the future, but for now we feel at home. It is possible that, even at an early stage of spiritual awareness, a seeker may sense beneath the different practices a reservoir of wisdom accrued over the millennia, a mystic love without division. (Chapter 14 will examine this concept more fully.)

Many men and women do not consider themselves an "anything", feeling that to pigeonhole their faith is to reduce it. Some, as we have discussed, are still seeking; others like the former monk have gone beyond the confines of a particular religious identity. I remember meeting a young Dutch woman who has set up home in India, not far from Dharamsala, and devotes her life to spiritual practices. When I asked her whether she was a Buddhist, she said, "Oh, I'm not anything."

Without thinking, I said, "Oh, you mean you are everything." And tendered for the first time the possibility that I too could be everything. We don't need a name or a label, or to fit into a pigeonhole: our faith is our own.

In reading Thomas Merton's *Asian Journal* and especially Bede Griffiths, I became aware of those who are able to move beyond their own faith. Both were monks in their own tradition; both were able to write from the inside about other faiths, both stretched their own religious identity to include something else. The French monk, Abhishiktananda, was very attached to the Church but expressed "the almost insuperable difficulty in finding a place for its forms and demands in what seems to well up in the mind as a direct result of the fundamental experience" (Stuart, 236). It is a struggle that many find between experience on the one hand and the strictures and structures of religion on the other. Many have been turned off by organised religions. A student of Warren's who has studied the Kabbalah for ten years ("I would not dare to call myself a Kabbalist") is so keen not to identify herself with a religious institution that she calls herself "a secular mystic". "You can't organise the Truth," said another interviewee. A mystic's experience happens individually, not institutionally.

In listening to men and women for this book, I have heard the richness and variety of spiritual journeys. The Spirit is dynamic; we may not believe tomorrow what we believe today, and many of the people in this book have passed through several religious affiliations before finding their current position. Such changes have not been shallow experiments with one religious practice after another but profound and often painful journeys.

Lucinda is a writer and leader of retreats and pilgrimages

both in Italy and in Toronto. For many years she followed a yoga path in Canada, with eighteen months "lying at the feet of Kwan Yin", then moved towards Christ within yoga as her guru. Lucinda's life is increasingly interior, monastic, mystical in prayer and devotion, and speaking less. She is part of a spiritual community of women, and prays regularly to Christ, the saints, Mary, and Sophia.

Jim comes from strong Roman Catholic roots which include attending a convent school and confirmation at the age of seven. At university he did a course in transcendental meditation, and practised regularly for some years. An interest in martial arts and Tai Chi developed into an interest in things eastern, and he remembers his first attractions for the monastic life in his early twenties. A personal crisis in his late twenties moved him back to Christianity, and he was baptised as an adult. Over the next two to three years his faith broadened and deepened from an evangelical Baptist position, and he became interested in liberation theology. At 38 he was ordained as an Anglican priest. Whilst training at theological college he attended a short course of meditation with the Friends of the Western Buddhist Order. As a curate in an Anglican parish he maintained a regular morning meditation. Influenced by the writings of Anthony De Mello and Thich Nhat Hanh, he started developing a practice of mindfulness in everyday life which he found particularly important in the midst of public worship, in baptisms, weddings and funerals. He still struggled with ritual and sacramental services, but found a personal meaning when remembering what he understood by the ritual of the Japanese tea ceremony. A five-day retreat in a forest monastery in Sri Lanka was a more recent experience which inspired a greater desire to explore the contemplative practices of the Buddhist traditions. Although moving into community life, he still recognises a great need to maintain a solitary and contemplative discipline.

After an initial intention of becoming ordained, Giles became a Franciscan tertiary in 1978. He is now the director of a Christian counselling organisation that he finds too evangelical. His spiritual practice is Zen, the specific teaching, Dogzhen of the Soto school. He became a student of Zen because he felt he wanted a deeper way of praying instead of just sitting without focus or discipline. If he has to have a label, Giles would call himself a Christian, although he finds clergy and the emphasis on dogma and the Bible suffocating. To call himself a Buddhist would, he feels, mean dealing with another set of moulds.

Giles is grateful that he is not a priest and, although he was romantically attracted in his teens to the idea of being a monk, he does not now feel that the clearness and purity of monasticism is for him. "I'm a family person. I'm more into the confusion of the world." He talks of the "spiritual abuse" of simplistic black-and-white religious views, the born-again "baby" who clings to certainty and cannot grow.

As we have found, many are without labels because they feel an allegiance to more than one tradition, or because they have moved through a series of practices, religious communities, to find a position outside or even beyond them all. David appears not to have had that struggle, but to have quietly found his own way forward. Now perhaps in his seventies, he has been a gardener for thirty years, and a mystic for as long as he can remember. He has always found mountains inspiring, and for some years worked as a climbing instructor; now too old to climb, he is not in any case, he says, so reliant on his environment for spiritual inspiration. He also worked as a teacher of "delinquent" children who "had crime beaten into them", and he decided that plants were easier. David has never married, realising that it was not for him, that he needed to live his own life, that he was too uncompromising. Life, he feels, is meditation, and much consists in unlearning what we have learnt about God, and getting closer to the essence. He has never felt the need for "a slot": God, he says, is the creative source which has all the possibilities. If we identify with a particular form we reduce the creative potential.

Krishnamurti went even further. In repudiating all formal religions, he said, "I maintain that truth is a pathless land, and you cannot approach it by any path whatsoever, by any religion, by any sect" (in Merton, 173).

5. ...BUT NOT OF IT

You never enjoy the world aright till the Sea itself floweth in
your veins, till you are clothed with the heavens, and
crowned with the stars: and perceive yourself to be the sole
heir of the entire world, and more than so, because men are
in it who are every one sole heirs as well as you.

Traherne, I: 27-31

*"On May 23rd 1999 I visited the Hindu temple in Neasden,
London. As I sat in the cool, white silence, I stared at the icons of
Lord Swaminarayan (thought to be an incarnation of Krsna) and
we had a conversation with our eyes. I felt completely loved and
understood. Minutes later I went downstairs to visit the exhibition
explaining Hinduism, and a priest showed me around. When we
were in a quiet place he asked me if he could touch my head. I felt
the most incredible heat, saw a blinding flash of white light and
it was as if he had transformed me into a different material, a
higher vibration. As I went home everything looked different and
beautiful, and life changed completely – I stopped eating meat and
drinking alcohol and started on an intense journey of purification,
knowledge and awakening.*

*"Since then I have grown from following the Swaminarayan
path in a very orthodox fashion to searching for any and all
mystical teachings and practices which resonate most strongly
for me. In January this year I was baptised (finally!) and
confirmed in a 'high Anglican' church which I attend regularly, but
I am also interested in the Quakers, Christian meditation and
gnosticism, Sufism, Kabbalah and paganism/earth religions. I feel*

particularly close to the teachings of Andrew Cohen who teaches about conscious evolution in relation to enlightenment, and seems to merge and build on the best of eastern and western religion. The journey feels like it has only just begun and when I have the energy (which is the biggest issue for me) I am enormously excited by this prospect.

"I also did a one-year healing course which showed me the importance of balance, which for me means a constant watchfulness over my tendency to avoid, escape or neglect the physical reality of being an incarnated human being on earth. I frequently wonder whether I should become, or indeed am, a nun.

However, I have also been involved in various types of activism and social work (just finished volunteering at a night shelter for the homeless, for example) and so the cave-dwelling life is definitely not my cup of tea. I would say that for me Jesus Christ is the ultimate (not only) spiritual teacher, and as I grow closer to God my heart expands, which brings me such joy but also some terrible pain in the rawness and openness. My aim in life is to become a decent enough vessel for God's love to flow through me in a way that contributes something towards the efforts of so many of us to create heaven on earth: I call it C.H.O.O.S.E; 'create heaven on our sacred earth'."

Primary school learning mentor, 37

A parallel universe

Of course we are in the world, and of it. We were born into it, live in it, interact with its suffering and its glories, both with other human beings and the natural world. To be "in the world" is to glory in the richness of life, our creativity, the variety of human talent and endeavour, as well as the infinite variety of the universe. However, central to the human condition is a feeling of restlessness, dissatisfaction, a hunger for stimulation, excitement; the feeling of a yearning, a void to be filled. The void is frightening; we do everything we can to cover it up, assuage our yearning. It is in dealing with this condition that we define our place in the world.

A friend said to me the other day, "I want something. I don't know what it is." She was talking of a desire not for a bar of chocolate but for something in her life as a whole: it was an unusually frank expression of this world dissatisfaction. Another friend, an entrepreneur, now a millionaire, is addicted to fast cars. He is now, in his late forties, racing them. The lure of danger staves off the need to contemplate the void. We can all think of ways in which we try to fill it: money, material possessions, ambition.

So what is it that we are trying to fill? What is all this shopping, noise, busyness for? Or the craving for a "relationship", success, a new car? Chocolate, cigarettes, alcohol or drugs? Strange how the void is never filled for very long, and demands more fodder to fill it. Sometimes severe illness – a heart attack, a stroke – will be the only message that gets through a destructive lifestyle. We are forcibly stopped, forcibly confronted with our own mortality and emptiness. As the void will never be filled by our own efforts, the only alternative is to accept it as part of ourselves and allow it to be. In my hunger for activity, I find I need to go through a period of "boredom", to accept it, to sit through it without filling it, for a transition to another state, approximating to what Thomas Merton describes below, to become possible:

> Contemplative life must provide an area, a space of liberty, of silence, in which possibilities are allowed to surface, and new choices – beyond routine choices – become manifest. It should create a new experience of time, not as stopgap, stillness, but as *temps vierge* – not a blank to be filled in or an untouched space to be conquered and violated, but a space which can enjoy its own potentialities and hopes – and its own presence to itself. One's own time. But not dominated by one's own ego and its demands. Hence open to others – compassionate time, rooted in the sense of common illusion, and in criticism of it.
>
> *1973*: 117

Only in that place can the deep hunger be met by deep joy.

For there is another realm, a parallel universe, a life not seen. A realisation of the spirit within is at the heart of our existence, and contemplation, a centring, a recollection, is an attention to that spirit. To allow that awareness to take place, there has to be an emptying, to make room. The less we hold of ego, the more space there is for the Divine; the less we push our own agenda, the more possible it is to change. This gradual transformation, this journey towards enlightenment, this trust in the unknown, and celebration of the grace that fills the universe, make up what we call the contemplative life.

Huxley expresses it thus:

> The divine Ground of all existence is a spiritual Absolute, ineffable in terms of discursive thought, but (in certain

circumstances) susceptible of being directly experienced and realised by the human being. The Absolute is the God-without-form of Hindu and Christian mystical phraseology. The last end of man, the ultimate reason for human existence, is unitive knowledge of the divine Ground – the knowledge that can come only to those who are prepared to "die to self" and so make room, as it were, for God.

(29)

To live sacramentally demands that we start with ourselves; with inner peace and love we can go forth into the world. To acquire and live with that inner peace we do not need to separate ourselves geographically, to isolate ourselves from the rest of the world. What is key is to cultivate the inner "monk", the monastery within. Sister Stephanie, who lives as a hermit in Tamil Nadu on a large and populous estate, defined hermitage as "silence in the heart. That is the true hermitage, the hermitage of the heart." Abhishiktananda, who lived in a material cave for many years, writes of "the cave of the heart". Sophie, who talks of "living with the sacred in daily life", also refers to a large space within.

Many I have spoken to have expressed this inner reality and the need to hold it while living in the world. But our attention is lived not only as an inner self-remembering but also in a glorification of the Spirit without. Thomas Kelly writes that we can live a life on two levels: "On one level we may be thinking, discussing, seeing, calculating, meeting all the demands of external affairs. But deep within, behind the scenes, at a profounder level, we may also be in prayer and adoration, song and worship and a gentle receptiveness to divine breathings" (35).

And it is that other realm, that parallel universe, that needs to shine through in our outward lives. We need "to approach the daily world from the prism of faith" (Dale, 51). The sacramental life in the world is not a compromise; it is a different experience lived with the same wholeheartedness as a monastic vocation: a dedicated life, dedicated to God and man. Those of us whose path is in the world are unenclosed, unprotected by a common identity and the values of those around us.

To live in the world is an explicit practical acceptance of the dynamic nature of the Spirit. Our relation with God is not in isolation of our fellow beings; as we are blessed, so we too are able to bless. The Spirit works on us to enable us to give something of what we have received to others, to act as a mirror. So it is that God works not only directly but through human beings, each on another. As we open our hearts and receive, so we give to and receive from other people. "To go to God one does not have to leave the people. On the contrary God is the God-of-People and can always be met in and through the People-of-God" (Pieris, 14). How we relate to the world and to other human beings is part of how we relate to God.

The former Buddhist monk, Wayne Teasdale, identifies four essential requirements "for successfully embracing a mystical path in the midst of demands of family and work: surrender, humility, spiritual practice, and compassionate action" (46).

Thomas Merton goes further. In rejecting the old notion of Christendom as a "world-denying society in the midst of the world", he says:

The world as pure object is something that is not there. It is not a reality outside us for which we exist. It is not a firm and absolute objective structure which has to be accepted on its own terms. The world has in fact no terms of its own...If anything the world exists for us, and we exist for ourselves. It is only in assuming full responsibility for our world, for our lives and for ourselves that we can be said to live really for God.

1980: 154

Living as a contemplative in the world is about taking that responsibility. We are mutually accountable for what after all is our world, a world not outside but part of our deepest self. It is not to live in abstraction. We are embodied. The incarnation in several religions teaches us of the inseparability of matter and spirit: our wholeness, integrity, groundedness are a crucial expression of who we are. Spirit without matter is as unbalanced as matter without spirit or materialism. Life in the world is about a series of balances: of the life within and the outside world; inner experience and outward witness; humility and using our full potential; being passive to God and active to the world; concentration on the present moment and with a view to the far horizon; time in eternity; this place in infinity. Joy and suffering; love and detachment; plenitude and the void.

In *The Path of the Buddha* a woman who devotes her life to working with leprosy patients writes: "My nature, though craving equally for asceticism and for social engagement, has to be dedicated to the latter while being supported by the former. This is a very delicate balance, never to be neglected" (Singh, 152).

Living as a contemplative in the world is also about accepting the here and now as our only reality, about building the Kingdom of God on earth now, not waiting for some future reality, not marking time till we come to a better world, or working towards future rewards or some concept of salvation. Whether or not there is an afterlife, whether or not reincarnation exists, "heaven" or "hell" is internal, now, causally inherent in our actions, not imposed by some external power.

Kshama runs a charity near Dharamsala in India, working in hundreds of local villages. She writes:

> I try to live Vedanta in life by trying to be alert to my self within and thoughts as an observer. To remain detached to the world with attaching to the Lord is my goal. This does not mean I do not interact with the world. It means being alive to the centre while being busy outside.

Frances used to be a professional ballet dancer. Brought up in Australia as a Presbyterian, for many years she had been absorbed in Eastern religions, cosmology, astrology, and particularly karma and reincarnation – the journey of the soul. Living in London, working as a dancer and also doing odd jobs to make ends meet, she went to her first yoga class. In the relaxation period, she found herself in a distant place, although aware of the teacher's voice. It took 20 minutes for the teacher to bring her back into the world, by which time the rest of the class had gone. It was an out-of-body experience and it changed her life. "Yoga found me," she said, "and everything fell into place." She has now taught yoga for some 25 years, and has become a yogini. "Ballet extended me outwards. Yoga called me home."

Taking a stand

Two snapshots:

The Dead Sea, Israel, 1990s, a man standing at the waterside, his family further up the beach, with a mobile phone tucked into one side of his swimming trunks and a gun in the other.

Oxford Circus, London, 2005. A loudspeaker blasting from the other side of the road: "Here's something to cheer you up. Come and buy..." while on this side of the street the tinkling sounds of tambourines and the chant of "Hare Krishna, Hare, Hare Krishna."

The society that we inhabit has in the main a secular viewpoint. To live a God-filled life in the West is counter-cultural. Even in a religious context, a contemplative life is seen as unusual, uncomfortable. If it is tucked away in a monastery with a recognisable identity and uniform, it is viewed as a comprehensible if eccentric way of life, but in the world anything more extreme than churchgoing on a regular basis or private prayer is incomprehensible. In the Indian sub-continent, on the other hand, religious life is so embedded in the culture of its citizens that all religious acts – bathing in the Ganges or sending flowers to sail down it, a *sannyasi* leaving his home to wander the world with a begging bowl – are viewed as intrinsic parts of daily life.

The word "worldly" suggests adherence to material satisfactions. So what are the values of the world from which we wish to distance ourselves? Spiritual writers have been uncompromisingly frank: "The traditional monastic understanding that one can be *in* the world but not *of* it can be reformulated as *engaged* in the world but *free* of it, engaged in the world and with others, but not attached to the world's greed, indifference, insensitivity, noise, confusion, pettiness, unease, tension and irrelevance" (Teasdale, xxiv); "fashion, habit, luxury, over-indulgence, greed" (Carretto, 76); "narcissism, pragmatism and unbridled restlessness (Rolheiser, 30). Pieris talks of this world being "a system of domination which we have created by our hunger for power" (88) and of needing to follow a model of service not domination. It is full too of exploitation, distortion, violence and a culture in the West and increasingly elsewhere in which we are all consumers and, even of education and medical care, customers. As Dale says, "We are the first society to be defined more by its modes of consumption than of production; the first society where shopping has become not a search for the necessities of life but a leisure activity" (55).

It's a daunting list. We are born into a particular age, a particular culture, and have to learn to come to terms with it in the best way that we, as individuals with individual gifts, can. So-called "worldly" values distort priorities. We know that on a daily basis our attention goes to possessions, security, to ephemera, the current trend, what's in, who's out, instead of taking a longer, deeper view, a view not pandering either to the urge to fill the void or the wish to conform to the values of those around us. Will it matter in ten years' time? Does it matter to people on the other side of the world?

All major faiths have an ethical dimension: they are not just a set of beliefs but a way of living that expresses a set of values. The eight-fold path of Buddhism, for example, asks for not only Right belief, Right attention or collectedness and Right contemplation, but also Right will, Right speech, Right action, Right means of livelihood, and Right effort towards self-control. "The values of faith", says Jonathan Dale, "are diametrically opposed to the values of the market...Love, truth, peace, community, equality point to an other-centredness wholly at odds with the market's relentless appeal to self" (59).

It is hard to behave counter-culturally, to make a conscious decision to bring up children without giving in to the pressures of advertising that bombard us all on a daily basis: the brand-name trainers, TV on tap. Adherence to fashion, to the appropriate brand name, denies our uniqueness. We reject what makes us special in the safe camouflage of "acceptable" gear. As a motto pinned up on a toilet door said: "The challenge is to be yourself when the world is trying to make you like everyone else." In the struggle to become who we are, often most acute in teenage years but for most of us a life-long battle, many people think of themselves as not fitting in, as outsiders. Perhaps that feeling is an unconscious connection to our uniqueness, instead of capitulating to the common effort to be like, and to be liked by, others. Living in the world is living in relation not from the narrow perspective of a fearful and excluding sameness, but from the position of our true selves. Our commonality is at a deeper level.

Christ called for us to become as little children; Buddhists talk of "a beginner's mind": an attitude of not taking things for granted, an innocence, naïvety, a child-like openness, which refutes the fashionable cynicism of the age. Living with a small child can help us learn the world anew, seeing its glory through the eyes of innocence. Cynicism is negative, deadening, shuts our eyes to the beauty of the world, the wonder of creation and our part in it.

The global communication of our age brings with it an access to unceasing communication. The ubiquity of the mobile phone: its jingle on bus, train and walking along the road betrays a need for connection, but an obsession with quantity overrides the quality of that connection. For a culture so obsessed with the coolness of "now", how strange it is that we do not actually live in the present. We isolate ourselves from our actual environment – the birdsong, a snatch of conversation – by ears plugged into a CD or MP3 player. Or, sitting at a restaurant table with a friend, when the conversation is not with that present friend but by phone with someone else, further away. We may be constantly "in touch" but with outer voices, not the voice within. There is no silence, no time or peace to listen.

Finding a creative balance between inward vision and outward witness is not easy.

In living our faith we are taking a stand for what we believe. In living a life that is essentially counter-cultural we are living at a critical distance from the values of those around us. The contemplative life has always had about it a strong element of dissent. It is not enough to be a mute witness; we need to speak it too. And this is where the danger lies. As soon as anyone believes that they "have" the truth, that can be the beginning of imposition, of oppression. What we are talking about here is making a statement with our lives, positing another way, standing up for the poor and oppressed, warning of the dangers and including in them our own weakness and fallibility. In witness to the centrality of love and justice we are in fact taking a prophetic stance against what we see as the inequities of our age. "Dissent properly arises from clarity of vision, from seeing things as they really are. It is rooted in truth. And it reveals the truth. That was the role of the prophets of the Old Testament" (Dale, 28).

This can be a tall order. In recognition of the fact that most adults spend the majority of their waking hours in a place of work, All Souls church in the centre of London considers it vital to have an active workplace ministry. It runs courses for "Christians @ Work"; for people working locally to discuss aspects of living as Christians in the workplace, as well as organising occasional events for specific occupational groups.

Dissent does not have to be on a heroic scale. Refusing a plastic bag in a supermarket, refusing to be complicit when invited to agree with a racist or homophobic comment: opportunities to stand up for human rights or economic justice can arise in any encounter of the day. "The choices we make in how to live our lives", says Dale, "are always more than they seem. They are a sign to the times" (27). We are not talking about life-denying puritanism or judgmental criticism of individuals; quite the contrary: our stand is to celebrate the joy of life and God's world.

The Quaker ROST (Recovering our Social Testimonies) group makes its position clear:

We recognise that our testimonies stand against many of the current strands of economic, social and political change. We are therefore clear that we have to dissent from fundamental aspects of the contemporary social order…We welcome the fact that our voices are amongst many which share such fundamental values. Together we need to dedicate ourselves to keeping alive an alternative vision of a society centred on meeting real human needs rather than ever changing desires; a society where inequalities of wealth and power are small enough for there to be real equality of esteem, a society which, mindful of the quality of life and the needs of future generations, limits its use of natural resources to what is sustainable; a society which is content with sufficiency rather than hankering after excess; a society in which justice is an active basis for social peace and community.

Dale, 10-11

Farley was brought up in the Southern states of America, the son of a Lutheran clergyman. In 1958 he escaped from a harsh home-life to Columbia University then to Union seminary, a hotbed of liberalism. It was a heady time, a time of social action, and Martin Luther King and Farley and his student friends were out on the streets. Nearly fifty years later, his dissent has taken a different path: his no less passionate commitment now is to the created world, for him "a religious imperative". He sees the world in the same place on this issue as with race relations in the past. "This planet's going to go. I don't want to live in a world where it's all gone."

At the age of 45 "Peace Pilgrim" (she wished the emphasis to be on her mission not on herself) began a pilgrimage that lasted until the end of her life at the age of 73. For twenty-eight years she walked 25,000 miles across the United States, carrying in her tunic pockets her only possessions, and proclaiming her message. "This is the way of peace: overcome evil with good, falsehood with truth, and hatred with love." Like the Indian *sannyasi*, her only food was what she was given, her only shelter what people she met offered her. Her walking, she said, was a prayer for peace. "If you give your life as a prayer you intensify the prayer beyond all measure."

Being "different"

How much to be in the world? In living a committed life, there are always adjustments to be made, if not compromises, but we do not need to conform. Do we need to own a property? Get a mortgage? Pay for insurance on our lives, on our possessions? When I left the publishing world, I was delighted to be able to let go of my daily newspaper, of the need to "keep up" with what was happening, in the close, voyeuristic detail with which we are fed the items of the day. Why is what is new so important? More important than what is unchanging? Reviews concentrate on the recently performed play, the latest novel, rarely a body of work. Papers, radio and TV are obsessed by "news". What is news? An editor's view of what people need to know, usually in the narrow context of national interest with a dash of celebrity. The emphasis is on "bad" news, on the negative: we know of man's inhumanity to man: it was ever thus; we need to work with the underlying issues, to concentrate not on the details of every occurrence, but on the changing of consciousness.

A group of young Quakers to whom I talked recently were fiercely resistant to this view. One, a journalist, talked of the importance of the press in uncovering corruption, the importance of keeping ourselves informed. For him and the others, active in politics, in demonstrations, in active dissent, the media fulfilled the dual function of informing them and giving them a voice.

As we have seen, those living in monasteries and convents

struggle with the being/doing balance. We have the same tension, but the balance necessarily will be different. Monks and nuns are "in" and wonder about going "out". We are "out" and wonder about if not going "in", at least about some form of distance in our lives.

Keeping that balance is not easy. Whatever our work, however fulfilling our family relationships, responsibilities make keeping enough time for quiet reflection difficult. Jan talked of a vivid experience that brought into sharp focus the tension between the different priorities in her life. Bringing up two children, juggling the everyday demands made on her, she was also deeply engaged in Buddhist meditation. Driving along the road to her meditation class, she was confronted by a young fox. She stopped the car, and found herself completely at one with the fox, boundaries dissolved, enveloped by the fear and dilemma of the animal in the danger it faced in crossing the road. When he had gone, she felt completely gutted, drained. She pulled into the side of the road to recover, and realised she could not continue meditation of such depth in a life with responsibility for children. She feels that to experience deep meditation you need to be held in community.

Most people have no choice about earning a living, tussling with the demands of everyday life, family and friends. Unlike monks and nuns, any distance that we create in our lives will be an individual not an institutional decision, and ongoing rather than once-and-for all. For us the context of life is largely unchanging; old friends and family may be bewildered by or unsupportive of radical change in someone they feel close to, indeed may feel threatened by what they consider to be an implied criticism of their own way of life. We cannot make changes without affecting those around us. All is connected. Relationships will be changed by the shifting priorities in our lives. We may no longer want to join colleagues in an after-work drink, or discuss the latest TV programme in the morning. Perhaps we no longer have a TV. One woman said that when she turned down an invitation to dinner because it was Easter Saturday, and she was committed to attending Vigil Mass, her friend of some decades' standing said with irritation, "Oh, you are always on your knees!" A couple living in a village with a good bus service said that neighbours didn't understand why they didn't have a car: "They think it's because we can't afford it."

A shift has taken place in my own life as faith has enveloped it, but I am blessed with friendships which on the whole have withstood the change in my career and mode of life. Perhaps my friends were more aware of my "real" self than I was; certainly the connections are deep and long-lasting. A childhood friend is now resident in Ireland and we were not in touch for many years. When I wrote some nine years ago to tell her I was attending Quaker Meetings, she said she had been doing so for twelve years. When I wrote recently to tell her of a meeting with an Indian Sufi and my subsequent reading of Idries Shah, she wrote that reading Shah had changed her life.

Being vulnerable

Living a committed life can be hard. The spiritual path is more perilous, more exposed, than the career path. Similarly silence is more exposed than a form of worship bounded by the certainties of scripted words or ritual. A religion where the rules are clear, the authority and institution secure, may provide an "opium", a safe haven, for its adherents, but those who stray into the realms of the numinous are taking risks. It is only by making ourselves vulnerable that we can be open to God's love. When you experience the relatedness of all created life as a daily truth, you cannot distance yourself from suffering merely because it is distant geographically. It exists; we are part of it. There is no other. It is perhaps not surprising that there is a prevalence of mental health issues among deeply spiritual people. In that sensitised state, some tip over the edge.

A former monk who fell ill and left his order spoke of an experience when "I lost ego-boundary, became Being, became all that I beheld; the sense of 'my' had gone. I was held transformed, watching my own watching of being. I became huge, experienced the cataclysm of the universe." He was, he says, profoundly ill, but now that he is better some of the experience has stayed.

My father too struggled with mental illness. One of the reasons it took so long for me to find my faith was because of an innate fear of taking off my blinkers and allowing myself to be open to the power of the Spirit. My father was a deeply spiritual man and most of his delusions were religious. With hindsight it is easy to see that there was a fine line between his illness and his spirituality; I did not want to follow in his wake.

It is easy to protect ourselves or allow being in the world to dull our sensitivities to pain, need and injustice. Living with an open heart is not easy. Sometimes, as the intensity of our awareness increases, we may feel a need to reduce the sheer quantity of input. It is simply all too much. Every impact is sharper, more powerful, both the joy and the suffering. The pain of a little boy clinging to his mother in love even as she shakes and shouts at him, the exhaustion of an old man climbing the steps of the subway, gasping for air, pierce the heart in heightened awareness, even as the rapture of cherry blossom or a rainbow, the transcendence of a late Turner painting. The world is full to bursting if we are open to receive it. How to harness this increased sensitivity, this increased capacity? How, crucially, not to be swallowed up in the suffering of the world?

The problem of suffering is the hardy perennial of spiritual life. With hindsight we can often see the lessons in our own lives – an acquired wisdom, a spiritual deepening, an increased awareness and understanding of others in their pain and grief. It is easy to discern the suffering caused by man in fear, ignorance, or for reasons of greed, ambition or distorted morality. Against these we can stand in nonviolent resistance and political struggle – whether it is physical violence against the person, economic violence against nations or ecological violence against the created world: cruelty to animals or the despoiling of the earth. But disasters of the natural world – earthquakes, tsunamis – or the death or suffering of a child, these we do not understand. Some will rail against a god who can allow such things to happen; others will try to analyse their causes. My own position is that we do not know, that in our present state of ignorance we see through a glass darkly. That does not mean acceptance, still less a fatalism that excuses inaction – just an understanding that we are human and not omniscient. We do not need to comprehend to be effective.

In the meantime we can express our common humanity in whatever way is possible, and go forward in trust.

Spiritual awareness not only opens our hearts in compassionate connection to the pain of the present, but also leads to the means of dealing with it. In holding a space within we will be able to hold suffering and detachment in balance, one of the many difficult tensions of the spiritual life. Only thus can we reach that balanced place that Buddhists call equanimity, and be given enough strength not just to cope, but to let our lives speak. In the following chapters we will look at some of the core issues for a life of faith, and some strategies by which we may be supported.

In 1999 I spent a month in Bangladesh. It was my first visit to a developing country, and I was asked if I was prepared for the culture shock. I knew that I was easily upset, but felt that I couldn't wear for ever the blinkers of a privileged life. The actual experience was quite unlike my expectations. In the event, what struck me was not the appalling poverty but the courage, resilience and dignity of the Bangladeshi people. The external view is always a distortion. It is in our impotence and frustration that the suffering of the world is intolerable. Only when engaged is our true spirit expressed. Only when we are faced by a situation can we know what we are able to do. For then the emphasis is not on *us*, on how we will cope with the problem of suffering, but on others and our relationship with them; in giving the Spirit its due, letting the love flow through us, we will know what we have to do.

"Everything matters; nothing matters."

****

Let's look now at some of the ways in which people support their life of faith.

6. LIVING IN COMMUNITY

Spirituality is about a communal search for the face of God
– and one searches communally only within an historical
community.

Rolheiser, 66

*Lynn is a retired teacher who has lived in community for much of
her life; it feels right for her, authentic. After a close contact
with one as a child, as an adult she spent seven years in one
community, twenty in another, both in East London. Both started
off with a social and political ethos, rather than a religious one,
though a number of the residents have been Quakers and she
herself attends a Quaker Meeting. The way of life in community,
including many years with a partner and bringing up her children,
"seems to make sense, rather than us all in little boxes". Now she
is living alone with a partner, and it is that that seems strange...*

To some extent we are all, even the most isolated hermit, living in
community. Even Tenzin Palmo, the English Tibetan Buddhist nun,
living 12,000 feet up in her Himalayan cave, was dependent on the
people who brought her food and other supplies from the valley
below. Even in the years when she saw nobody, supplies were
left for her. The Indian *sannyasi* who has renounced the world
deliberately makes himself dependent on the local community.
Local people, recognising his role in supporting their spiritual
needs, play their part in supporting his needs of the body. A self-
declared solitary, living in the world, will live in the community of
her neighbourhood, engaged socially to some degree in the give

and take of shopping, public transport and other social services. Few isolate themselves entirely from friends and family. For monastics the residential community is key. "Stability" requires a commitment to staying in one place, with the same group of people, for life. The checks and balances of living with others, the expression of love, the discipline of observing vows in community, and the richness of a shared prayer life, are fundamental.

Regular attenders at a church, a mosque, a synagogue, will have their religious communities: like neighbours, companions not chosen but a salutary check of individual ego; conflict providing opportunities for milestones of learning. Living, as Richard Rolheiser puts it, within "the muck and grace of actual church life" (66).

In some societies, living communally is the norm: in extended families, with neighbours, sleeping, eating together, sharing possessions. Solitude or privacy can be viewed as a privilege or indeed as abnormal. Society in the West is largely made up of people who live in small family units or, increasingly, alone. The number of one-person households has been on the increase over the past few decades as people choose not to marry, not to have children, or as they live longer, they outlive their spouses.

At a practical level a residential community provides company and can also be a pooling of resources that is not only ecologically beneficial but helps solve the difficulties of living on a low income. It enables a way of life that does not have to be focussed on earning enough to pay the rent or the mortgage for a separate establishment. It can allow men and women to live creative spiritual lives, perhaps working as volunteers or in modestly paid jobs in the caring professions.

Hartrigg Oaks is a purpose-built community estate for people over 60 which opened in 1998. It comprises over a hundred and fifty bungalows, and a 42-bed nursing home. The community centre has community rooms, a restaurant, spa pool, shop, library, internet access, and has self-run societies for over thirty different activities. It employs about a hundred people. Most residents pay a set sum when they move into a bungalow, and this sum is returned when residents leave Hartrigg Oaks. Residents do not own their house; the whole estate is owned by the Joseph Rowntree Foundation that built it. About a third are Quakers, and about a third are from military backgrounds.

But buildings do not a community make: one of the residents, Peter, estimates that just under half the 230 residents do consider it one; the others simply want to be looked after. Despite the facilities, as in any society, there is loneliness. There is too, as in any group of older people, a consciousness of death: Hartrigg Oaks is, Peter says, a place of "creative ageing".

Living in community is more than a convenience: it involves taking responsibility and can be a small example of our wider interconnectedness. For some it is a way of life that provides a necessary and visible counter-balance to the excessive individualism of the modern world. Community structures will also, to some extent, deal with some of the issues about how much to engage with the world. In some, the residents will work outside; in others the work is entirely for the community, in growing vegetables or running courses and meditation.

Some communities are grounded in worship, governed by a rule, a communal ethos, a way of life expressive of a spiritual code that all members have in common, a practice of living together in love and respect, of mutual giving. There is an intimate connection, says Patricia Loring, between our interior life and our communal practice: worship, mutual care and service, corporate structures, support in counter-cultural life.

The Othona Community in Dorset comprises about half a dozen resident core members, and includes work, worship, study and play. This centre describes itself as "rooted in the Christian heritage...open to the wider future". Othona has another centre where it began on the Essex coast. An inclusive approach is long established: "The Othona Community was brought into being and is sustained at its heart by faith in God through Jesus Christ, but it welcomes and learns from people of every belief and none, and their involvement is needed and essential as part of its function and structure. Without them the community would not be fully effective."

Communal worship at the Dorset centre takes place once or twice each day. On Thursday evenings – in a distinctive Othona practice which dates back to the 1940s – there is a recitation of names of those present and those to be remembered in prayer. The ministry of the centre is based on its hospitality and spiritual teaching, with a busy schedule of courses or visitors for 290 days a year. "Community" says the warden, Tony, "is whoever is here at the moment."

Michael, also at Othona, has lived in community much of his life, firstly at Laurieston Hall, an early commune, political rather than religious, but with guidelines for living together. When we spoke he was about to move to co-housing in a farmhouse to live with a group, "connected by the Spirit and with a higher vision" but not committed to the kind of outreach offered by Othona. He has not wanted to live alone but feels the new move is a half-way house. For Jim, too, community has been an important theme since his days in youth work. As an ordained priest, he has worked to reconcile Buddhism and Christianity in his life. He feels moving to community is an important living out of values and beliefs but admits it is difficult for someone who is also a strong individualist.

Tony has been keen on community since student days, feeling it is "a natural process of all I hold dear". He has seen the development of the centre, enriched by the differing spiritual paths of the core members and with space to express their interests. As a result there is now, he feels, an increased sense of warm acceptance at the heart of the place. Such a fluid approach to community living avoids the tensions that often arise when the responsibility for decision-making is in the hands of non-residential trustees.

In active communities like Othona for which hospitality is an important part of the ministry, it is inevitable that there will also be a tension between meeting the needs of the resident members and those of its guests. For resident members of the Iona Community – who welcome over 100,000 visitors a year – it is a major consideration. Each community will have to look at the balance, and provide ways of safeguarding the coherence of the resident community as well as individual needs for time alone.

The Bruderhof movement is based not on hospitality but on the family. Based on early Christian communities in first-century Jerusalem, and on similar movements in sixteenth- and seventeenth-century Europe, it began in Germany in 1925 and now flourishes in USA, England, Germany and Australia. The whole family is catered for. Children are an important part of each community and participate in most communal gatherings. Disabled and elderly members are cared for within the community. The largest Bruderhof has over four hundred members; the smallest has about twenty. But each one follows the same daily rhythm, and has the same basic departments, including a nursery, kindergarten, school, a communal kitchen, laundry, various workshops, and offices. Shared meals and communal work are an important part of daily life. No Bruderhof member receives a salary or has a bank account. Income from all businesses is pooled and used for the care for all members, and for various communal outreach efforts. Manual skills are valued and encouraged, though technology will be used where useful.

The goal of the Bruderhof communities is to create a new society where self-interest is yielded for the sake of the common good and are open to all who strive for justice and peace, no matter what their religion. The only rule is that there should be no talk against any brother or sister. Without this rule, they feel, there can be no loyalty and thus no community.

****

There is a danger, perhaps, of communities creating a distance from the rest of the world, of not being truly "in" it. Some want, perhaps, to create a small Utopia, protected and isolated from mainstream society. On the other hand, they may make a statement to the world to proclaim difference and to engage with it from that stated position.

A Quaker intending to set up a community writes:

It is not just about living in the same house together, but building the inner core so you as a group can go out to, or bring in, the wider community in a more meaningful way than as an individual.

She explains that their intended way of life will definitely include

worship together; we're not really keen on set rules, we think it is important to have one's own space for when you need it. Probably everyone should be a stakeholder to give commitment and a way out without wrecking the whole thing. Also some contribution to the community living in a hands-on way. A freeing of resources – time, talents and finance. A simpler existence – more self-sufficiency, sharing of property. A little more of being a Quaker in the way early Friends would have understood the bonds between Friends!

Sophie, a young dancer who describes herself as an engaged Buddhist, lives in a self started community: "We can live like this with little money, creating a valid structure." It is, she feels, important to empower people to move away from convention.

We aren't an intentional community I don't think! In that we don't have a rule/contract/mission statement. It's pretty loose. We use consensus. We do have a commitment to each others' heart and spirit growing. We don't have a common practice though the original founding group did the 5 rhythms dance practice. Half of us have this still.

We have a commitment to communicating, to sharing, to

supporting each other on our path. The general mood is playful, heartful, affirming, allowing of pain and joy, creative, expressive. We meet formally together once a week, we share how we are, we share practical tasks, we share cooking, we have a "talking book" in which we daily share practical and emotional issues, frustrations, conflicts, hopes; we sometimes meditate together, sometimes play games, sometimes make music, sometimes go out together.

Another member of the community said, "It's like a good house share – perhaps a bit more structured, supportive." Then, after consideration, he realised there was more to it and said, "It's subtle."

So what is an "intentional" community? The following definition, from the website www.ic.org seems to contradict Sophie's view:

An "intentional community" is a group of people who have chosen to live together with a common purpose, working co-operatively to create a lifestyle that reflects their shared core values. The people may live together on a piece of rural land, a suburban home, or in an urban neighbourhood, and they may share a single residence or live in a cluster of dwellings...A group of people who share values, goals, commitments, and hopefully living space and food. A group of mutual respect and support.

The Hengrave Community was founded in 1974 and, until it closed in 2005, comprised about 20 volunteers of as many nationalities:

Christians, of different denominations and walks of life, both lay and monastic, "committed to equality, justice and service. Recognizing that we have different gifts, we value equally every kind of contribution made to enrich our common life. By working together and helping each other, we hope to make a difference in this divided world."

Eleanor, who lived at Hengrave for five years, wrote:

If our communities are inclusive, they become tiny models of what Christian community can be. An intention expressed by a member of the Hengrave Community at the outset was that the community might be a model of the Church of the future: "a model not in the sense of being perfect, but like you make a little sketch: not perfect, although you always hope things will be good". The community was to have "a fuzzy shape" and be willing and able to change. Such inherent openness can go against the grain of our natural human tendencies.

She is frank about the difficulties of living in community.

I remember occasions when I wished those around me would quite simply go away. I'm quite sure that the feeling was mutual. There were other times, of course – by far the majority – when I could recognise my fellow community members as a blessing and know that the whole we made together was greater than the sum of its parts. This is where the balance and pattern of community life are so important. Rules surrounding silence can baffle an outsider, but it doesn't take long when one lives on the inside to appreciate why such rules are there. Living above the shop with over twenty others, I was eternally grateful for silent Hengrave breakfasts which ensured questions about bookings would only come up after my cornflakes.

"The mark of real community", a friend said after using the toilet, "is whether on using the last sheet of loo paper, anyone bothers to replace the roll."

Another woman living in a small ecumenical community says that she feels that she has lived in community all her life – that living in a family or with others is no different. After her husband died she decided to join a community. She said she was bad at human relationships and wanted to learn how to live with others. "If you live alone, you do not bump up against other people."

Community has been defined as a group of people with whom we have not chosen to live, and living in community can be a hard discipline. It is not easy to acknowledge that the person whom I find most difficult may be the person who can teach me most. Living with other people, seeing ourselves in the eyes of others, is an important way to self-knowledge. Conflict is part of the human condition, and in recognition of that communities will often build in methods of conflict resolution – nonviolence – to the ethos of their life together.

A community does not have to be geographical. A loving bond of common values and practice can sustain individuals even when living apart. The Iona community, an ecumenical group of men and women "seeking new ways of living the Gospel in today's world", was founded in 1938 to break down the barriers between prayer and politics, between the religious and the ordinary. Its 260 members and 1500 associate members from many backgrounds and denominations are scattered throughout Britain, with a few overseas. The men and women, both lay and ordained, form geographical "family" groups and are bound by a common five-fold rule of a daily devotional discipline, sharing and accounting for their use of time and money, regular meetings, and action for justice and peace.

Pat has been a member of the Iona community since 1979. She lived and worked on the island until 1982, and was the co-ordinator of the prayer circle for five years. Originally a social worker, she was drawn to the emphasis of the community on faith in action and its roots in the slums of Glasgow. She values the sense of belonging and the routine of daily prayer for each other, building relationships even with those she has never met. Action too keeps the scattered community together and provides a framework that challenges her to do not just the work that she wants to do.

On her regular visits to the island Pat enjoys leading services, especially those for healing, though she has no aspirations to the priesthood. As a Roman Catholic, Pat is aware that although the community is ecumenical, it tends to be viewed from a particular standpoint. She spoke of the importance of respecting different groups and not measuring all by a Church of Scotland yardstick. The community works closely with those of other faiths; maybe in the future the links will become closer.

In his essay "The Blessed Community", Thomas Kelly has written of a wider concept of community, a special connection that binds all those who "have seen the light", have found faith, are on the path. We will return to that subject more fully in Chapter 14.

Note: for those wishing to join a community in the UK, there is a very useful little guide, *Digging and Dreaming: The Guide to Communal Living*, that has been reissued for 2005/6.

7. SPIRITUAL DIRECTION

Giles is a Franciscan tertiary and the director of a Christian counselling organisation. As well as his counselling work, he acts as a spiritual director for several people. He looks forward to retirement so that he can take on more clients. His own spiritual advisor is a Zen master, so he has the unusual experience of two traditions of direction from different standpoints. Giles says that they are very different but in general he prefers just to allow the two to lie alongside each other. "Zen", he says, "abhors all comparisons!"

When pushed, he said: "Christian spiritual direction and Zen guidance happen at a slightly different level." The Christian method emphasises "accurate discernment and a rational way of taking decisions. The meeting with a director might take an hour or even longer.

"In Zen, spiritual direction (Dokusan) is solely focussed on helping the student to let go of attachments and delusions (i.e. everything!) It is centred around a special relationship with the teacher, whose purpose is to bring the student into an immediate experience of the Essential World... and this is always grounded in the limitless potential of the here and now. It can only be experienced within, and does not invite any theology or indeed any thinking. One Zen teacher has suggested that most religions seem to point the student away from himself and towards God: whereas Zen – which is not a religion – points the student to look for the Truth deep within, where there is no Subject and Object.

"The teacher may challenge the student, sometimes quite fiercely, and the Dokusan meeting may last only a few minutes, at the end of which the teacher rings his or her bell, sending the student

back to his meditation cushion in the Zen hall."

Not everyone feels the need for spiritual direction. Indeed, one of the priests interviewed for this book felt that all of life was his teacher: "the robins, the mountains, this conversation is spiritual direction". Matthew Fox, former Dominican monk and author of, among other books, *The Cosmic Christ*, says that his spiritual director is his dog. The world outside and inside is our guide.

For some it will be a necessary step at a stage of their spiritual path. Sophie, an engaged Buddhist, currently has no teacher though she was guided in the 1980s by Western nuns and monks returning from the East. Others feel the lack of direction and perhaps do not know where to look. Sarah, a former postulant, misses it, although her experience of it among Catholic chaplains was "not impressive": she found them "proud and controlling". One man, sexually abused by a priest, was too suspicious of anything connected with authority to consider taking on a director.

In general there has been a considerable increase in spiritual direction. Given the growth of the "unchurched": those people seeking a spiritual life outside the confines of a particular faith; those who find the dogma and structures of orthodox religion a barrier to the expression of their faith, rather than a spiritual home, it is not, perhaps, surprising. For those without a natural religious community, the need for occasional support, a check to see if they are going in the "right" direction, is common. Even for those within, say, the Christian church, with official support links, the need is increasingly there. For priests, the bishop may not be a sympathetic listener; for members of the congregation, the priest may be a distant figure; all may simply be too busy to spend time with an individual and her spiritual path.

The master

The guru or spiritual master is a sacred figure in Eastern religions.

Despite the distortions of contemporary popular culture and some exploitative money-making enterprises of the 1960s onwards, the highly trained, disciplined figure of the guru in Hinduism, the *murshid* or *Shaikh* in Sufism, the master, teacher in Buddhism, is an indispensable mediator for many of the religions and mystic traditions of the world. Even a Tibetan Buddhist hermit has a guru. Mata Amritanandamayi (Amma) and Sri Ramana Maharshi are rare examples of people in the Hindu contemplative tradition who have not. It is said that Sri Ramana Maharshi had undertaken spiritual direction in a previous life. The importance of the guru in Hinduism is underlined in the Upanishads.

In essence, the guru is considered a respected person with saintly qualities who enlightens the mind of his disciple, an educator from whom one receives the initiatory mantra, and one who instructs in rituals and religious ceremonies. From generation to generation the institution of the guru has evolved various basic tenets of Indian culture and transmitted spiritual and fundamental knowledge. Gurus formed the axis of an ancient educational system and ancient society, and enriched various fields of learning and culture by their creative thinking. Herein lies the lasting significance of gurus and their contribution to the upliftment of mankind.

hinduism.about.com/ website

Complete obedience is required from the disciple, often over a period of years.

Daria in Louisiana has been ordained as a priest in the Vedanta tradition, has recently been called to take *sannyasa diksha* and has already begun the initiation. When I asked her why she needed a guru, she wrote:

This is a question that other people frequently thrust in my face because I have been so devoted to my guru for the last 16 years, and because I have willingly relocated myself on more than one occasion at his beckoning, leaving behind friends and loved ones to do so. So the question is always "Why do you need him? Why are you giving your power away to another person?" Sri Swamiji himself even teaches that you don't need him, that you are your own guru...so why bother?

A guru/devotee relationship is a strange thing. People come to gurus for all sorts of reasons, some of them not spiritual – such as gaining material possessions or because they see themselves as gurus and want to gain power. Others inherit their guru. He/she has been the family spiritual leader and they have been raised to follow this guru. Others come because they are in a philosophical/religious crisis. And others come because they have dreamt of the guru, or had a vision of him and find him. Still others, like myself, are found by him. He came for me. I didn't know I was consciously looking for a guru. But when I met him, and he told me that he had come for me because I was ready for him, I knew he was speaking truth. When you are ready, the teacher does come!

An important thing to understand is that not all devotees

really belong to the guru. A "true" devotee is one who has been incarnating with the guru since the beginning – whose energy/vibrational pattern is karmically/perpetually connected with that of the guru. Rarely, does the guru say who true devotees are. I was blessed in that Swamiji told me from the beginning that I was one of his true devotees, and I know deep in my soul that that is true. However, for about 99 percent of devotees, this question, even if asked, is never answered out loud. That's why people are often going from ashram to ashram in the east seeking their "true" guru – looking for that "soul" or vibrational connection.

If you have that connection, it is like finding a soulmate. It's that simple. It is a love affair of sorts. I don't mean that in sexual terms in any way. But the heart to heart connection is intense, and it can be all consuming at times. Still, why a guru? Well, one important reason is because if you are going to become truly enlightened, you have to learn to surrender and to serve. Many people who are on a so-called spiritual path are seeking power, but few really understand it. Most are not willing to put in the long hours of hard work on oneself it takes to surrender your ego. Of course the paradox is that the more you surrender, the more you self-actualize and come into your own power. The guru will keep you surrendering until you fully learn to serve – first him/her, then the immediate community, etc. etc. etc.....when you have come to the realization that to be a master is to be a slave to others then you are taking your first baby steps to being on your own. Your guru will always see greater gifts in you than you see in yourself...and that alone is enough reason to stay....

Another woman compared the process to therapy. The subject matter of sessions might be different, but she feels the process of transference is the same, which is why some turn against their gurus. Without a specific spiritual home, her journey was moving on quickly, and she felt it likely that she would always want the stimulus of a teacher – not always the same one – in her life. From the point of view of the master, a Sufi teacher told me, "The 'master' at best is a 'mirror'; to be 'used' in the right manner possible. After that whether it is 'cast away' or 'destroyed' or 'venerated' is of no consequence to the mirror."

Transmission

The transmission of wisdom through a lineage of masters from one charismatic teacher is a central concept in Eastern religions. "Lineage and tradition", says Kornfield,

> are the sacred containers for preserving practices and wisdom that have been discovered and accumulated over generations. Lineages are the form through which the light of awakening is passed from one generation to the next...When we choose a teacher, we are drawn into the powerful current of a lineage and partake of its worldview, its visions, its possibilities and its limitations.

(237)

• **Zen**: In her memoir of her path to become a Zen priest, the Rev. Roshi P.T.N.H. Jiyu-Kennett writes movingly of her preparation for and receiving of the Transmission from her master. As a foreigner in Japan and as a woman, she underwent considerable ordeals to reach that stage and went on to be one of the first Western women to become a Zen Master and an abbess of her own temple. Giles, who came to Zen some eleven years ago, confirms the importance of the transmission of *dharma* from enlightened master to disciple.

• *Hindu*: In India, Kshama, too, regards the lineage of her master, Swami Chinmayananda ("Guru Dev"), from his teacher, the influential Swami Vivekananda, to be of the utmost importance. Even Ramakrishna, the founder of so much that is modern in twentieth-century Hinduism, set great store by the continuity of his teaching: the original inspiration and power are maintained through an unbroken succession of spiritual teachers.

• *Jain*: Priha's guru is from a whole tradition of gurus stemming from Srimad Rajchandra, a poet living in the early twentieth century, and an influence on Gandhi.

• *Sufi*: "The Sufi teacher is the link between the disciple and the goal. He embodies and symbolizes both the 'work' itself, of which he is a product, and also the continuity of the system, the 'chain of transmission' " (Shah, 351).

• *Tibetan Buddhist*: Transmission is also believed to take place by reincarnation. *Rinpoche* (precious one) is the name given in Tibetan Buddhism to one identified as an incarnation of a previous master, an incarnation often recognised in early childhood, from when he will be trained, often in great austerity, in the ways of the master.

Dependence

The early Judao-Christian tradition did not rely on spiritual masters. In early Christianity the parish or monastic structure provided the kind of spiritual guidance necessary. Only when monks went out to the desert as solitaries in the fourth century, did the need for spiritual directors become necessary. Such direction was simple but profound, the Abbots giving advice usually not ordained. Interestingly, St Francis and St Clare acted as each other's spiritual director. From the beginning directors were aware of the dangers of dependence. Desert novices were to let go of their spiritual father when considered mature and able to live under the direct guidance of God. Other traditions also recognise the importance of non-permanence. Eckhart Tolle gives clear advice: "Nor must you come to depend on a teacher or master except during the transitional period, when you are learning the meaning and practice of presence" (88). In Sufism the relationship between Shaikh and disciple is seen as a temporary stage in the disciple's life. "The man of wisdom is initially the guide of the Seeker. As soon as possible this teacher dismisses the disciple, who becomes his own man of wisdom, and then he continues his self-work" (Shah, 122).

The purpose of spiritual direction
What is the purpose of spiritual direction? First of all, whatever the similarities, it is not psychoanalysis or therapy. Opening up the spiritual life may help emotional problems; a director will certainly get to know his directee as a whole person "in the concrete circumstances of his life" (Merton, 1975:16); but the purpose is specifically to work on his spiritual life. Thomas Merton defines it as "a continuous process of formation and guidance, in which a Christian is led and encouraged *in his special vocation*, so

that by faithful correspondence to the graces of the Holy Spirit he may attain to the particular end of his vocation and to union with God" (*ibid.*, 15). Its purpose is "to get behind the façade of conventional gestures and attitudes which he presents to the world, and to bring out his inner spiritual freedom, his inmost truth, which is what we call the likeness of Christ in his soul" (*ibid.*, 17). This definition may serve more widely than for Christianity.

The objective is to help people to grow into the precious individuals they have it in themselves to become. Each path is unique; each destiny too will be so: an offering of the gift that is hers alone to give. The uncovering of that gift, that real person in all its entirety, is the ambitious aim of spiritual direction. A director needs to see us as we are in the eyes of God, our real self; speaking inner truth, the action of grace in our souls.

The important thing to understand is that a guru doesn't teach everyone in the same way. Swamiji constantly stresses that what works for one devotee to help them in their spiritual development may not be good for another. It is his decision what is best. What I have come to learn over the years is that you don't always get what you want. But you do get what you need from your guru, and always when you need it. Understanding that your guru is not a wishfulfiller, but a spiritual master is an important lesson along the way.

Daria

The danger of isolation recognised by the early Desert Fathers is particularly relevant in our contemporary fragmented society, especially in a context when many do not find the confines of one religious tradition meets their needs. For those in a mystic tradition, without the grounding of a religious structure, the way can be hard to find. "The Sufi personality cannot mature in solitude, because the Seeker does not know exactly which way he is heading, in which order his experiences will come" (Shah, 346). In this context it is important to mention the limitation of language. Our usual terminology is often misleading. The word "path" indicates that there is a direction to follow, a linear experience of travelling from A to B; in reality the experience is not linear but – and it is only possible to talk in metaphor – spatial: an expansion, encompassing; a movement of the heart. Sufi teaching will depend on the recipient's ability to receive.

Several of the people I spoke to have a relationship with their guru or master at a distance. Both Priha and Daria, living in England and the United States, respectively, have gurus in India. Both try to visit once a year and communicate by email. Kshama's two gurus are no longer living. She differentiates between them thus: "Param Pujya Swamiji is my Guru. I was fortunate to be in his presence for short periods from 1985 to 1993. Being with him, hearing his discourses, having opportunities to meditate with him were my directions. Swami Chinmayananda whom we called Guru Dev lives in my heart. His teachings are alive to me. His guidance is there once I close my eyes and think of him."

Frances's discipleship to Swami Satchidananda ("truth, wisdom, bliss") was as part of a group; she never had a one-to-one relationship with him. He left his body in 2002. "I don't grieve for him as a physical entity. That would mean I had lost the plot. It's a test." Her guru embraced all religions. He would use the numbers on a watch to indicate all the main religions of the world, with the number 6 representing the religions of the future – the ones that have not yet been invented.

When asked about spiritual direction, the Kabbalah teacher, Warren, referred to his companion and mentor, his spirit-guide, his *magid*. Some years ago, feeling a presence, he asked, "Who are you?" The answer came: "Someone like yourself, a writer." He asked, "Do I have any of your books?" and was led to the only book his father had given him, by a great mystic and teacher of the eleventh century. He feels the presence come when he needs an answer.

A director may provide not only clarification for the student but an outlet for the sharing of deep experience. He might provide too a necessary connection with a community of which he himself is a part. For ecumenical or even interfaith directors (a recent development) the community will be less narrowly defined, a part not just of one religious community but of the larger community of faith (see Chapter 14).

Forms of spiritual guidance

Spiritual direction in any faith can take many forms. Where the role of master is central, the model of direction will tend to be authoritarian, the guru, master, teacher revered as a representative of God on earth, himself taking on a god-like status. In India, the shrines of spiritual leaders such as Ramakrishna, Sri Ramana Maharshi, Sri Aurobindo and his disciple, The Mother, are surrounded by devotees praying and making obeisance.

The spiritual master is to be honoured much as the Supreme

Lord because he is the most confidential servitor of the Lord. This is acknowledged in all revealed scriptures and followed by all authorities.

Prabhupada

Guru is Shiva sans his three eyes,
Vishnu sans his four arms
Brahma sans his four heads.
He is parama Shiva himself in human form

Brahmanda Puran

Complete obedience, even worship, is demanded of the disciple. Even Ramakrishna "bound his disciples to him for ever...and welded them into a single family".

The dangers of infantilism in this kind of relationship are evident. The Mother, in a refreshingly wry reflection on all the prostration around her, responded to a disturbed journalist's question: "Mother, are you God?" with "Yes, and so are you."

In other traditions directors are seen in a more modest light. If not as representatives of God, on what authority do they act? "The only authority they can have is the authority of their own persons as people who belong to [the] Lord and to his community and who seem to take seriously their own relationship to him and his community" (Barry and Connolly, 137). Shah makes a similar point: the task of the Sufi teacher "is in being, being himself; and it is through the proper functioning of that being that his meaning is projected" (348).

Although, as Josh has found, the two may be the same in practice, Thomas Merton makes a clear distinction between the role of a director in the Catholic church, and that of a confessor or supervisor. Obedience is not due to a director; he is not a superior. The image in general is more of a guide, a mentor, someone accompanying another on their adult journey, an experienced person, a designated listener, seeking guidance from the Spirit within. He is the one responsible for keeping the focus on the Spirit of God, mirroring back, asking hard questions. One of the Roman Catholic women I talked to said that she relied on "two very good friends, one a religious Sister and one a priest, who help me reflect on my daily experience and where the voice/hand of God might be in that. This helps me a great deal in terms of deepening and living my faith and developing my sensitivity to Christ's call."

Unexpectedly, one of the best guides to spiritual guidance comes from an American Quaker, Patricia Loring. Quakers, with their testimony to equality and their lack of intermediaries in worship, find such guides acceptable, she says, only if they are named by the community or asked for by the directee – not if they put themselves forward for such a role.

As in the rest of their spiritual lives, those seeking their own path will experience the need for spiritual guidance as an inner call rather than an externally imposed discipline. Such guidance may well be felt necessary for a particular period in a seeker's life, a moment when clarification is needed, or a when the seeker is moving on to a higher stage of development. The ancient tenet held in martial arts as elsewhere: "When the disciple is ready, the master appears" is an experience known to many, and it may be the only way in which a teacher can be found. Sufi masters, for instance, do not proclaim their identity and are often working in commonplace activities in the world. In some schools the disciple must prove her commitment and removed from the world but in conscious relationship with it, to be engaged in life and with people. At ease, unafraid of life, patient, self-confident, tolerant of strong emotion, even anger. The process itself demands privacy, confidentiality and time.

Ultimately, it is important to remember that the process is a holy one, an opening to and interaction with the Holy Spirit/God, whatever name is appropriate for the culture. "We must never forget", says Merton, "that in reality we are not taught by men."

This point was also made by some of the people I talked to. For one woman: "all the adversities and synchronicities are our real teachers"; another wrote:

On a [Native American] vision quest, everything is guru. As you sit out there in the wilderness, you study what is about you, and wait to see who/what comes. No matter what is there, or what shows up, it is your teacher in the Native tradition. If you've had a good quest, ultimately you realize that your vision doesn't stop and that your life is always your vision quest unfolding.

Abhishiktananda says that

for the Vedantin there is only one guru, the one who shines, not-born, in the depth of the heart. The external guru is only the temporary form taken by the essential guru to make himself recognised, and at the moment of that recognition there is no longer either guru or disciple…The Christian guru is never anything but the manifestation of the Lord.

Stuart, 238

8. SPIRITUAL PRACTICE

After living for several years in a war zone in former Yugoslavia, Sophie found that with her level of emotion the container of her Buddhist insight meditation practice could not hold her. She needed a different approach to allow the intense energy to move through her.

5 rhythms dance, Sophie says, is about freedom and connection. It is a spiritual practice and an expression of purpose in community. The practice is to communicate and to receive emptiness; to be present and empty. There is no pushing; the dancer is the servant of the dance. The nature of energy is that it goes through different stages; to allow the cycle to happen fully, it is necessary to get out of the way. Sophie describes the dance as exploration, playing, and witnessing each other with kindness, emotional nakedness and sexuality.

She used the metaphor of a wave to describe the stages of the dance:

flowing: continual movement, receiving, feminine;

staccato: the forming of the wave, the beginning of form, direction, beat, masculine, doing, shape, structure, repetition;

chaos: breaking of the wave, surrender, the end of form, conflict, letting go;

lyrical: crashing on the beach, bubbles, playful, space, imagination, new idea;

stillness: pulling back into the water: prayer and stillness, integration. During the dance the person can be centred and still.

Sophie practises communally twice a week for up to six hours and alone in personal practice, as well as attending week-long workshops. She also returns to former Yugoslavia for a month each

1. Reading
2. Discursive meditation: maybe reflection on reading
   a) projection
   b) examen
   c) examination of thoughts in the present moment
3. Journalling
4. Prayer:
5. Meditation.
6. Retreats
7. Listening to each other and being heard: This she describes as a transformative experience: "the pivotal discipline between personal and corporate practice" (see Chapter 7 on spiritual direction).

Other practices that people find helpful include walking, dancing, drumming, *hatha* yoga*, T'ai Chi – a variety of activities, sometimes the main focus of a spiritual life; sometimes a small part of it. Wayne Teasdale writes: "My life of prayer contains many elements: contemplative meditation, *lectio divina*, the practice of nature, including walking meditation and sky meditation; contemplative study and reflection; and allowing for silence and solitude" (24). Many use *pranayama* or breathing exercises. Peter's breath is a statement of his purpose: he breathes in his gratitude: "thanks", and breathes out his intention: "yes". Cora supplements her churchgoing with joining a Zen meditation group

---

*The term "yoga" is more than the Western understanding of a form of physical exercise. The yogas are the five principal disciplines for achieving union with the Absolute (see Chapter 9).

for two hours every week. Gwen has a quiet time on waking before "entering the world" and enters into spontaneous prayer throughout the day. For Jains sleep is a spiritual practice: in sleep we do no harm to the created world.

Let us examine some of Loring's suggestions further:

Reading

There is a different way of reading spiritual writings, not in a cerebral way but with the heart. Called *lectio divina,* it is an ancient monastic practice that can transform the manner of our absorbing what we read, whether the sacred texts – the Bible, the Koran, The Bhagavad Gita – or other spiritual writers that are found to be useful. My own experience is that one leads to another; one writer refers to or has influenced another; our own need moves on and is excited by different writers at different times. Like Simone Weil, I am "obedient" in my reading, devouring only what I am hungry for, often an affirmation of a recognised truth. My own practice is to read in the early morning. The discipline of not putting on the radio, delaying the process of opening up to the world for an hour or so first thing in the day, is important to me, and starts the day in a way in which I wish to continue. Farley too reads first thing in the morning – in his case the Bible and *Quaker Faith & Practice* – and he does not answer the phone. As a Jain, Priha's reading is her main daily spiritual practice, and she is examined on it before moving on to the next stage.

Examen (Examination of Consciousness)

This is a key part of the discipline of the Jesuits. A typical prayer is an exercise in self-awareness. Ignatius gives five steps:

Praise and Thanksgiving

Petition for Light,

Examination of Conscience,

Expression of Sorrow and Repentance,

Resolution to be more faithful to God (a personal internalisation of the Eucharist).

Examen has been taken up as a useful practice by many outside the Catholic church. It can be a form of looking back over the past twenty-four hours, keeping an awareness of the presence of God in our lives, "monitoring God's activity in me as a matter of habit" (Pieris, 113-7). Loring gives us a form it might take:

"Where have I met and co-operated with the Spirit today?

Where have I met and evaded the Spirit today?

How do I speak to God about this?"

Or

"Where was Love today?

How did I miss it? Meet it?"

For the Benedictines practice is structured by the **Liturgical Hours**. In *The Music of Silence*, David Steindl-Rast has offered lay readers a beautiful exploration of this way of worship, and the qualities and demands of the different hours of the day.

Journalling

This practice has become increasingly popular and the subject of a number of courses. Keeping a journal can be regarded as a record or as a meditation in itself. It can be an account of the presence and work of God over a lifetime; it can be a more immediate prayer journal. My own is something of all of this, though it often lapses into a less spiritual dimension. Crucially, like private prayer, it is between ourselves and God; it is an opportunity – not always easy to take – to be unselfconscious in our examination of the whole of ourselves, including the dark sides. Another Quaker told me that her journal plays the part of an "examination of conscience". Sometimes it is a clarification, sometimes a cry for help in trying to cope with hurt or inadequacy. "I don't find prayer easy," she says, "but writing can be cathartic, in the best sense...There is a definite awareness of a deeper presence as I write...even if I don't voice it I don't feel I'm alone as I write."

Prayer

There are probably more questions about this subject than any other part of spiritual life. What is prayer? Loring describes it as talking to God, intentional communication. She calls intentionality our ultimate concern, part of the unification of the divided self, and defines it as "the relationship of attraction between ourselves and what draws us".

Prayer can be divided into several different types. Active prayer is that which begins with a human activity, which can include visualisation, chanting, images, ritual symbols and mantras, which then might lead to meditation. Formal prayer can be analysed, as Pieris says, according to structure: time of day, frequency, duration, place, posture, order and method; it can also be vocal or mental, personal or communal.

In terms of content, Christian prayer is usually divided into petitionary (requests for self), intercessionary (request for someone else), contrition, and contemplative (see Chapter 9). We might add "praise" or "adoration". Burrows talks of the importance of our involvement in any intercessionary prayer that we make, the cost to us. In other words, if we pray for somebody, it is not enough to sit back and let it happen. We need to take responsibility for our part in what happens, to allow ourselves to be instruments of God's purpose.

A lot of people have a problem with prayer, even monks who talk of going through the motions, and the difficulties of keeping mind and voice in harmony. It is even more of a problem for those who do not have a tradition of liturgy or ritual, and for whom prayer is usually mental and often personal. (The Quakers are unusual in having a largely silent worshipping practice that is communal.) Such problems are nothing new. St Paul admits: "we do not know how to pray as we ought but the Spirit himself intercedes for us with sighs too deep for words" (Rom. 8:26, RSV).

I have struggled with the idea of prayer, feeling it unhelpful to "pray for" someone or something, when all is known to God in any case. As Dag Hammarskjold caustically remarked: "Your cravings as a human animal do not become a prayer just because it is God whom you ask to attend to them"! Words seem singularly inadequate – my only vocal prayer is *in extremis*, when I might call out in spontaneous appeal. (Perhaps that is the time when I come closest to God.) At the same time I do believe in the power of focused positive thought or feeling, and have found useful the definition of prayer as "attention", holding someone or something "in the Light". Steindl-Rast is helpful: "Prayer is not sending an order and expecting it to be fulfilled. Prayer is attuning yourself to the life of the world, to love, the force that moves the sun and the moon and the stars" (xvii). Dom David Morland talks of a common human condition: "Prayer is not so much a matter of words or ideas but rather a deep, inarticulate longing for one in whom one's whole being can rest and be at peace" (Boulding, 71). In the end, perhaps the most helpful advice is: "Pray as you can, not as you can't."

Meditation

A word needs to be said about the different understandings of the word in the West and in the East. In the West meditation is usually active, often guided or on a particular image. In the East it is either an emptying, a letting go of any discursive idea, or giving one's whole attention to a formless thing, using a *koan* (enigmatic Zen saying) or mantra. In the Soto school of Zen Buddhism, particularly, having a goal is seen as an interference. The *zazen*, "sitting", is to attain clearer awareness of the moment.

Insight meditation is an all-encompassing practice, a way to healing, purification, detachment and awareness by concentrating on different parts of the body, or pain of the mind or heart. In that stillness, we may be confronted by what the Buddhists call "the three poisons": craving, hatred and ignorance, which sum up aspects of our negative thinking, and need to be understood and assimilated. Practice is built up over a long period; steadfastness and concentration are the keynotes. "To learn to concentrate we must choose a prayer or meditation and follow this path with commitment and steadiness, a willingness to work with our practice day after day, no matter what arises" (Kornfield, 57). What is required is a willingness to let go of everything and go to the centre of our being.

Vipassana meditation is an intensive and repetitive practice of developing mindfulness. The form it took in the Thai monastery that I visited was individual repetitive and timed meditation, walking or sitting slowly and mindfully, stopping to acknowledge any distraction such as an awareness of the senses or a movement of thought, by naming it: "hunger, hunger, hunger" or "itchy, itchy, itchy" until it has passed. No guilt is attached, no sense of "failure", merely an acknowledgement and a new beginning. Ten minutes walking; ten minutes sitting, then starting all over again. Gradually the sessions were built up until each was for half an hour and included some variations. After hours of meditation, I found myself deeply resistant, exhausted, wanting to run away but pushing myself further, through a barrier, and sometimes into mystical awareness: an intensification of normal life. I was then reminded of the importance of transience, of not allowing myself to be attached to the experience. For Josh, living in Rome, regular Vipassana retreats remind him of his Indian heritage; Michael said Vipassana meditation "took me to a place where I looked at my fears". The work he did enabled him to realise that "I am not my fears."

Chant

This is an important part of practice in many traditions – from Buddhist to Benedictine. Jill, who has practised and taught chant for many years, says that the listening is more important than the sound you are making. Her speciality is Mongolian or Tibetan overtone chanting, a form which makes audible the higher harmonics from a note when it is sounded. The pure high sound of overtones is very "democratic", seemingly detached from the individual making it, like the music of the spheres. The vibrations from the practice affect the whole body in a subtle form of work-out. The Benedictine Steindl-Rast gives a view of the significance of chant in another tradition. "Chant embodies both impermanence and endurance. Not one note lasts more than a second or so. Chant is movement and change. And yet the continuum of chanting through all rhythmic and melodic changes conveys a quality of permanence and timelessness" (85). "Its rhythmic tranquillity becomes embedded in your soul. You carry it with you all the time, wherever you go. It creates an interior monastery" (101).

Music plays an important part in many traditions. In Sufism, for instance, when words fail, it is common to turn to the sound of the bamboo flute or the vibration of a stringed instrument. Even non-religious music-making is connected. I am a trained singer and try to practise daily. A friend of mine commented on my wish to sing out of earshot of others. "It is your spiritual practice." It had not occurred to me till then, but song often lives with me through waking moments, and even at night when I might dream I am singing, or a tune is with me as I wake. God's gift, embedded in my soul.

Retreat

A retreat is about silence and stillness – stillness of the spirit as much as of the body; silence of the mind as much as of the tongue. We need this silence and stillness to step away from the bustle of doing and to re-familiarise ourselves with being, and in fact the deepest part of our being, the soul, is silent and still.

The peace and serenity we have been searching for lie within and are always there – it's just that we've forgotten that this is what we are. A retreat will help us re-discover this and cultivate a truly spiritual awareness of the self. Once we have experienced this higher consciousness, the consciousness of the soul, and learned to re-connect with the eternal self, we can then move out again to the life we've stepped away from, adding new purpose and meaning to it and the way we connect with others and the world.

Brahma Kumaris' World Spiritual Organization website

Retreats have become big business. Increasingly men and women are turning from the stresses of everyday living in search of a quieter time. Websites are burgeoning with details of a variety of retreats: yoga holidays, Jewish retreats, interfaith retreat centres world wide. The Retreat Association lists some 250 mainly Christian centres in the UK. If you add to that the numbers who seek solitude on an informal basis, and those going to India or a Greek island for a yoga course, those taking career breaks to explore a spiritual path, the numbers are significant.

Retreats may take the form of courses in various aspects of the spiritual life in a retreat centre, or may be a largely solitary personal retreat in a monastic setting. Retreats will normally be for a week-end, a few days, possibly a week or two. More unusually, and more seriously, there are longer retreats. Traditional within Tibetan Buddhism is the three-year retreat during which it is common for adherents to take temporary ordination. According to the International Association of Yoga Therapists, "Long retreat supports the cultivation of deep equanimity and empathy for others. Absence of these qualities perpetuates mistreatment of people and the environment. The work of transforming self-interest into concern for the welfare of others is critical to creating enduring peace in our world."

The Gandhi Foundation Summer School in England is a multi-faith annual family retreat, a temporary community expressing a Gandhian way of life. The days are structured to include instruction, physical labour, creative activities such as spinning and relaxation. The food is vegan, accommodation is either in single rooms or dormitories (on the floor). Gandhi's life and example, and the theme of nonviolence, are naturally to the fore.

A time on retreat is time "out", away from the routines and responsibilities of daily life, as well as communication from the outside world. Two women told me of retreats that they were leading, one in the UK, one in Italy, in the week of 9/11. There were no papers, radio or TV for the retreatants; each leader decided not to interrupt their peace, telling them only at the end of the week of the atrocities that had taken place.

For those attempting to live a committed life in the world, some periods of retreat from holding life in that balance are valuable, in many cases a necessity. For Giles, "hermit" periods – after an initial longer period, normally a week per year – are seen as the third leg of a spiritual life made up of being a Franciscan tertiary spiritual director, and his Zen practice. Several of the North American women interviewed for this book join together for an annual retreat. Multi-faith, the predominant traditions of this group are Shamanic and Roman Catholic, its emphasis on loving service and the power in the world of the feminine.

I have recently visited a centre of Christian spirituality, based on Benedictine tradition, with meditation held morning and evening, and open to people of all faiths and none. The founder, Dorothea Pickering, is pictured in a photo in the sitting room with the Benedictine monk, Bede Griffiths, who established a Christian ashram in India. She wrote, "We are an interfaith as well as a meditation centre. It is at the level of silent meditation that we are on common ground, attentive to the God Who is infinitely without, yet wholly within."

What I have discovered there is a little "hermitage": a hut, about 6'x10', with a bed and folding table, on the River Thames in the corner of a large garden of a communal house. The first night, alone in an unlocked hut accessible both from the garden and from the waterside, I was a little nervous, thinking of a human intruder or a rat. The next day, elated in the freedom of the little space, I realised that by facing our fears, however insignificant, we make spiritual progress in our search for complete trust. The hut is not mine, it does need to be mine, but I hope to return on a regular basis, to be surrounded by birdsong and the changing seasons.

Simon has his own hut: built in his garden, of recycled materials, it is both a workshop and a quiet place to which he tries to retreat each day. Others have allotted places in their homes as "sacred spaces" or "altars". In Louisiana, Gwen's table in her family sitting room overflows with candles, feathers, dry flowers, shells, scarves, boxes and china with motifs that have a spiritual significance for her: the moon and the stars. In London, Warren's "temple" too is abundant with pictures and symbols of life and death, the cosmos, Adam and Eve, symbols of celebration of the universe and all in it. His wife has a little Tibetan shrine in the attic. Such places are intensely personal, each reflective of the life and faith of its owner. Others, like many Quakers, will have no such place, believing that no place or object is more sacred than another: the whole of life is sacramental. A place of retreat is of course an external context for an interior experience, and it is not necessary to go to a special place to find that experience: indeed, for people in the world, although a reprieve from daily struggle with noise and busyness may be welcome, it is essential that they find such peace in the context of their daily lives.

The natural world, the wilderness or desert experience, forms a large part of answering the need for replenishment of the spiritual life. Several women I have interviewed have been influenced by the Native American connection with the land. Jan talks of "The Green Song": something she feels everyone used to be part of. Far from the sounds of traffic and machinery, in the stillness of the natural world, the voices of mice, flowers and bushes can be heard. "We sang it too," she said. "This is our song." And that tuning into the universe is something that she wants to be part of again.

At the age of 50 Simon took a career break. Setting off on Easter Day without a map, he took three and a half months to walk from Budapest to London. He had been prepared for the walk by an older wise man who acted as a mentor, and encouraged him in "awareness and praise". It was a life-changing experience. Walking he found was an external manifestation of the inner experience.

Simon talks of opening up to the reality and richness of the world, rather than dry meditation. On his three-month walk "an Alleluyah occurred" – and he can now draw on it at any time. Sophie too expressed a need for wilderness; she finds it hard to keep the large space in her heart while living in the city. Peter has a hut in the mountains, to which he retreats from his priestly duties.

The joy in creation, realised as a child, has been the rock in his life, the one constant that has never gone away.

I too have found that confining my spirit in highly disciplined rituals of meditation can have a depressing effect, that it does not make use of all of God's grace. It is in the natural world, especially in the large expanses of elemental landscapes – mountains, the desert – that my spirit expands. Uniting with the created universe is heady, liberating, a confirmation of my ministry being in the world. Each path is different, and each needs to find her own.

****

Many I spoke to do not have a regular formal practice. Some are daunted by the idea of practice, do not know where to begin. As one of the people I spoke to said, many in the West are now allergic to devotional ritual. They have been alienated by the "mechanical" prayers of their childhood, the repetition of pre-scribed words, not spoken from the heart, the imposition of church attendance and of what are to them empty forms of prayer. Even if the content is acceptable the regularity of the practice is felt to be sterile. For Simon, even the effects of the Christian meditative practice that he otherwise found helpful were negated by the imposition of a twice-daily routine. If an external pressure to conform is not matched by an inner impulse, the likelihood is that the practice will be empty of real significance. Simon needed the spontaneity. For him the important moment was "when my mantra rooted itself in my heart – and it's never stopped. At any moment I can go inside and reconnect with that rhythm."

Others expressed a regret about not having a regular practice – it was something they would like to develop, either when they made more time for it or when they found something significant for themselves. Uncomfortable with set forms of words or ritual, they had not yet found their way to something acceptable. Mike, for instance, has no regular personal practice, but would like it. He finds it hard to find a prayer focus that is acceptable, but sometimes goes into church before work or at lunch-time for a period of quiet. A Methodist who loved singing but was increasingly uncomfortable with the words she was singing, had recently found in a local Taizé group a communal practice that spoke to her condition. ("How do Quakers sing hymns?" "Slowly, because they are always looking at the next line to see if they agree with it!") She had herself been several times to the ecumenical Christian centre in France and found their simple repetitive chants beautiful and helpful in her life.

The purpose of practice

What is important is to remember what all this practice is for. Not for its own sake. Abhishiktananda talked of the danger of being "lost in techniques". A former Catholic told me: "I wish I had more discipline. But I can get caught up in too much of that. I loved the regularity of services and ritual." Burrows reminds us: "Our methods, the scaffolding we use to support ourselves, must never be confused with prayer itself or given much importance." The attention needs to be not on ourselves but on God. "We must watch...that we are not trying to control our prayer. That is the danger with all our methods...[using] them as barricades behind which we can hide, defending ourselves from God. In practice this means protecting ourselves from feeling inadequate" (99).

When we find that a practice, however useful in the past, has become mechanical, when it no longer comes from the heart or expands the moment, it is time to reconsider. I have been twice to Taizé. The first time was a powerful experience that moved me on in understanding and spiritual maturity. The second time for whatever reason, it left me cold. It was not the right place for me at that time. Our spiritual life, our awareness of self and of God, is not static. The Spirit is dynamic and moves in us – if we listen, our understanding and our practice move accordingly.

Sri Ramana Maharshi said that there are two ways of approaching God, to be chosen according to our own nature – the way of rigorous self-inquiry, or complete surrender of all responsibility for one's life to God. The distinction between surrender and effort is a subtle one: the concept of grace is to be found in Buddhism but is more central to the Christian attitude which emphasises not only our effort but being in a state of receptivity so as to be found by God.

There are many who feel that the contemplative life cannot be maintained without punctuating it with regular formal practice. Lucinda feels that if you do not do practice regularly, faith cannot deepen; it needs the discipline, even if not at set monastic hours. Loring agrees: "Although the Spirit will work in our lives whether we are 'present' or not, it is difficult to sustain our own intention…without such a regular reopening and reinforcement" (8-9). And Burrows: "It is hardly likely that we shall enter fully into the sacramental life, receive the transforming action of God, unless we set aside some time exclusively for prayer" (95).

A friend who has been practising Hindu meditation for many years was asked by his father: "But what are you practising *for*? Will you never achieve it?" One answer, said my friend, is that the lifetime's practice is for one moment, that final moment of death. Another answer might be that practice is to prepare us for *life*, for bringing our increased wisdom into the world

9. MARTHA OR MARY?

"i don't see contemplation as the opposite of action, if action is seen
rightly. i see contemplation as bringing the emptiness and silence
and stillness that underlies the immediate world into our immediate
world – to hold the two together, although they are not really two at
all, it only seems so. if we know the world from within contemplation
then everything is one** and action is simply what emerges in the
moment. (**well it is one whether we know it or not, but you know
what i mean!)"

John, organic baker

Contemplation

In the previous chapter we looked at the various types of formal
spiritual practice. We look now at informal practice, what might be
called contemplation.

Prayer is to prepare ourselves, to open ourselves to God's will,
and make ourselves channels for God's love, the Spirit. "To pray
contemplatively", Burrows says, "is to abandon one's idea of how
and why it all works...to trust in the living presence and reality of
the divine...to accept a place in a living process whose end or shape
is beyond our comprehension" (65). In that sense it is a passive
state, and many testify to the feeling of not so much praying as
being prayed through. We do not pray to affect God but that we
ourselves might be changed in the process. One woman talks of
wishing to be pure consciousness, like a rain stick without the
obstructions.

From the previous chapter it may seem that anything can be
prayer – and that is the point. It not only can, but needs to be. To

live our faith is to try to live constantly in the presence of God, to keep that awareness in all that we do, and that is without exception the aim of the people in this book, indeed the criterion for their inclusion.

* "Wherever there is love, there is only prayer. When our heart is in the right place and brimming with love, everything becomes prayer." (Steindl-Rast, 78)

* "In the midst of our work, we should retire within ourselves, even if just for an instant, to recall Him alone who keeps us company." (Teresa of Avila)

* "This Way consists of continuous worship in every action, both external and internal, with complete and perfect discipline according to the Sunnah of the Prophet." (The Naqshbandi Order of Sufis website)

To live like that is our aspiration

Peter: Though a priest, he has no formal personal practice. "I am living my faith all the time. God is relationship; God or love is in the giving of a cup of tea to a homeless person, the stopping of a fight."

Priha: When I commented that it is possible occasionally during the day to collect oneself to an inner space, Priha's response was such an echo of Thomas Kelly's description of two-level living: "Oh, I try to do it all the time."

Sarah: contemplation is in the every day, on the tube, doing the washing up, and with her partner. "All the things I thought would take me away from contemplation, actually bring me to it."

Gill: Although it is important to find times of non-busyness, the whole of life is worship, including encounters. Of her artistic activities she said: "painting is using the energy in me, almost personalised. Poetry is now my spiritual autobiography. A creative network of veneration."

Tony used to chide himself for not having the kind of regular practice he had been encouraged to admire, then realised he worshipped in his own way. He is more at home in the universe than he used to be, and described his spirituality as an oceanic sense of the Divine.

Mark: "Ultimate reality is here. We don't have to do anything except breathe to understand who we are. There is breath. We are part of breath."

Warren describes his life as being in the present all the time. He sees the face of God in everyone. "God wishes to behold God and we are the eyes and ears of the Holy One observing all that is going on."

Being present

Practice can be such a small matter: a pause for gratitude before a meal; indeed a pause before embarking on any activity, to make its intentionality clear; a pause during the day to take stock, centre ourselves. In that pause, like the moment between one out-breath and the breathing in, or between a wave receding and the swell of the next, is a space of another dimension. During mental prayer or meditation, just the act of gently brushing away random thoughts is a spiritual one, a declaration of priority and intention. Taking things slowly and deliberately is hard for me: my inclination, my old habit, is to do several things at once, rush at what I am doing – eating, washing up, cleaning – to get it over with before going on to the next thing. But what am I rushing for? Or to? When all is finished I find myself in a state of needing something else to put my energy into.

I have to work at being mindful; concentrating on one thing at a time. When I broke my dominant arm recently, not only did the restriction give me an insight into the lives of those who manage permanently with one arm, it also slowed me down. All my attention had to be on the task literally in hand: putting on a jacket, opening a tin, carrying the bowl for breakfast and then going back for the mug. It enforced a mindfulness that had been lacking in the fall that caused the injury.

Being in the present moment is all that we can be. The past has gone; the future is unknown. But we are rarely present in this moment: still, aware of the totality of the experience. Being in the present is not to deny the past or ignore the future. In our dreams we sometimes make contact with something beyond time, either in a "preview" of something to come, which we perceive as a *déjà vu*, or we experience a different sense of time within the context of the dream itself when past and future seem melded in a present action. These always seem to me intimations of the artificial emphasis we put on time. We run our lives according to the clock, yet have a relative attitude to its inexorable regularity. We are "short of" time; time seems to be going quickly when we are enjoying ourselves or getting older, slowly when we are bored.

"Eternity is not a long, long time. Eternity is the opposite of time. It is no time. It is, as Augustine said, 'the now that does not pass away' " (Steindl-Rast, 8).

In mystical peak experiences it is commonplace to be held in a unity of time and eternity, place and infinity. When we are stilled, present, in the moment, when we allow eternity to enter our lives, the relentlessness of the clock and of our lives loses its power and we can begin to approach such moments of fruition. There is a story of a businessman going to an African country, and rushing from meeting to meeting. Someone says to him: "Ah, you in Europe have all the watches; we have all the time." Time is not a limited commodity but an elastic series of opportunities and encounters.

The word "present" relates to place as well as time. Being present, living "mindfully" is about living more consciously, with more awareness. We might like to resuscitate the obsolete definition of "present" in the Oxford English Dictionary as "favourably attentive". How often do we sail along on automatic pilot, our minds on what we have left behind or what we are going to: worries, concerns, anticipations, regrets? This preoccupied way of living means that we cannot be present to other people either – viewing individuals in terms of their role in our lives: bank official or receptionist instead of human beings with needs and private lives.

Our lack of presentness is often to do with the repetitive nature of our lives. I remember thinking (with self-congratulation) that my daily commute to London was like being on a conveyor belt: my mind could be elsewhere. Instead of such abstraction we need to be aware of "the capacity to witness the unfolding of our lives" (Elgin, 149). The present moment is a gift and our awareness of it leads to gratefulness and joy. "The boundaries between the 'self-in-here' and the 'world-out-there' begin to dissolve as we refine the precision with which we watch ourselves moving through life" (*ibid.*, 152). Not only has time not run away with us but we feel the richness of that moment, an awareness of all that there is, and our connection not only to God but to the Godness in all that surrounds us.

The popular view of contemplatives is that they are absent-minded. The reverse is true. They are present-minded. The systematic practice of mindfulness, based on *satipatthana*, a discourse given by the Buddha, is central to all forms of Buddhism. Mindfulness is the awareness of what one is doing while one is doing it, and of nothing else. The four "foundations" or areas of awareness are: of the body and senses, the heart and feelings, mind and thoughts, and awareness of the principles that govern life. Kornfield emphasises the centrality of this concept: *"The development of awareness in these four areas is the basis for all of the Buddhist practices of insight and awakening"* (42-3).

The practice of mindfulness is extensive, not only in Buddhism. "Recollection" and "self-remembering" are also expressions of bringing the self back to an awareness of the present moment. In a God-centred faith, that recollection will be to the Spirit within and to God's will. *The Practice of the Presence of God* is a slim volume of letters and conversations describing just that: a way of life in which everything is done for the glory of God: an active title for an active expression of our faith. Brother Lawrence, a seventeenth-century French lay brother, spent years washing up in the monastery kitchen, every moment consecrated, in the present and in the Presence.

For such people there is no distinction between worship and

daily life: all are one. Simple, and the hardest thing in the world.

Silence

Silence is a mainstay of monastic routine, and an important tool in the spiritual life. An inner stillness can be aided or reflected by a stilling of the tongue, and a cessation of communication in any form: by phone, email or letter. It has surprised me in some Christian monasteries to see monks writing each other notes to avoid, in a purely literal sense, breaking the monastic silence. In the stillness, the mind and heart turn inwards towards the spirit within; it is a place of listening, of waiting on God. Silence is after all where those in closest relationship are at home – there is no need for speech. A Quaker Meeting is a collective experience of this kind: a listening for a presence that might be mediated through any one of those present in spoken ministry. For many the need for such stillness spreads into a larger part of life. Spoken prayer for me would be an oddity: my personal as well as my communal practice is in stillness, and in silence.

A silent day on a recent retreat imbued actions with increased care and deliberation. The decision to be silent in a group is more powerful than in solitude, not just an absence of speech but an intentional and listening attention. Gyan told me of a silent retreat he had attended some years ago in Australia. A friend of his passed him a note which said, "Are we being silent, or are we trying not to talk?"

Darkness

In my flat there is a small place of complete darkness. In a city with the glare of street lamps that is hard to achieve, but in this small space it is possible to sit on the ground, back against a wall, with eyes open and see nothing. Like the vast featureless spaces of the desert, that "nothing" seems full: of infinite potential, infinite space. Visual silence. The darkness does not close in, rather the spirit expands towards infinity. Shutting our eyes, as many do during worship, will remove visual distraction and aid the journey within, but sitting in the dark with eyes open can extend that realm beyond the boundaries of self.

The dark is a metaphor for our unknowing, and proceeding in that darkness is an expression of trust, of faith itself. It is not surprising that "trust" games usually entail shutting our eyes and relying on others to lead us, or catch us as we fall. Walking in complete darkness can be frightening. A friend once suggested that we allow ourselves to experience the darkness in a night-time walk between two villages without street lighting on a cloudy moonless night. As we switched off our torches, I was anxious, debilitated by fear, ostensibly of bumping into something, tripping over a hole or a root, but perhaps more profoundly of the unknown.

The dark is also a place of growth. In the darkness of the earth plants germinate, seeds develop, fallow ground is renewed. In times of darkness and seeming lack of progress, the internal work continues. We can sometimes look back on periods of seeming sterility to find that that fallow time was necessary for later growth. In creative activities, it is often the pondering time that is most fruitful; solutions to problems can often appear without effort after a good night's sleep. Like the "compassionate time" of Thomas Merton, the periods of darkness, dryness, passivity, can be a springboard for inspiration and decisive energy. Not for nothing is the turning point in mystic experience described as "the dark night of the soul".

The movement from darkness to light and back into darkness is the common rhythm of natural life and it is also a spiritual rhythm. God is a hidden God, both knowable and supremely unknowable. Movements of intellectual awareness are movements into the light, movements of intuitive awareness are movements into the dark.

Boulding, 97

I value my time in darkness, my not knowing, even my pain, as I then simply have to abandon myself to God.

ibid., 106

Play

When a Sufi friend came to a Quaker Meeting for the first time, he appreciated the silence and the way that spoken ministry arose organically from it, but remarked that we were a gloomy lot. He expressed the wish for a "mirthquake" at our next meeting. It is true that we in the West tend to be rather earnest. There is a humour and sheer good nature particularly among Buddhists – think how often the Dalai Lama is seen chuckling.

But it is more than humour: there is a lightness of being that comes from self-awareness and freedom from the goal-seeking that is so prevalent in our culture. If we enjoy the moment, with no thought for what arises from it, then play becomes possible. A few years ago a course of clowning evening classes showed me another way of being. The concepts of innocence, play, and above all a trusting goal-lessness, were instrumental in a way of working that allowed the natural course of events to occur rather than pushing to make things happen.

A particular exercise sticks in my mind. Two of us were asked to start off from opposite corners at the back of the stage, and to imagine that there was a very special shoe at the front that we both wanted. We were silent, and only allowed to move when the other one did. After a while, the other clown was far further forward than I was. The teacher shouted: "Jennifer, you're f***ed!" In desperation I began to indicate the existence of an even better shoe at the back of the stage, and the other clown, joining in the spirit of the game, went back excitedly to look for it. I, still goal-centred, rushed forward to gain my prize. Of course, there was no point in it – it wasn't even funny. How much better to forget about the original goal, go back and join in the game. Alan Watts expresses it well: "This is not a philosophy of not looking where one is going; it is a philosophy of not making where one is going so much more important than where one is, that there will be no point in going" (145).

The clown or fool in Shakespeare's plays is often the channel for wisdom, a simple naïvety cutting through the nonsense of received wisdom in the circles of power. The concept of "holy fool" occurs in many traditions – particularly Sufism and Zen, with its many stories of the fool Nasruddin, whose "foolish" behaviour points to the hidden truth.

* * * * * * * * * * * * * * *

As we have seen, there are some for whom formal practice is a necessity, while others feel its regularity to be artificial, mechanistic. Is it laziness? Or acknowledging the unpredictability and spontaneity of the work of the Spirit in our lives? Each will find her own answer. The thing to remember is that what we feel is not relevant: "True prayer takes place in our inaccessible depths. Anything we experience can only be a sort of backwash of it, either joy-giving or painful. It is unimportant" (Burrows, 102).

Martha or Mary?

How marvellous to be without and within, to embrace and be embraced, to see and be seen, to hold and be held – that is the grace, where the spirit is ever at rest, unified in joyous eternity.

Walshe, 84-5

One whose life is essentially interior, a "monk in the world", often feels inadequate, guilty at not "being out there and doing things". Ironically, the Marthas of this world also feel guilty: that they are too busy, not spending enough time in silence and solitude. Both may be true, though guilt is beside the point. Although the general reading of the Biblical story is that Mary was the more "spiritual", Meister Eckhart suggests that it was Mary who had much to learn, which is why she needed to sit at Jesus' feet. It was after his death that she began to serve. Martha, however, was already able to work from the ground of her being. She "stood maturely and well grounded in virtue, with untroubled mind, not hindered by things" (Sermon 9 in Walshe).

An individual inclination may be more towards action or contemplation, but we can work towards a life that is more inclusive, more in balance. Robin, in Louisiana, is doing so.

Brought up a Mormon, and now strongly influenced by the Native American tradition, she has retained the notion of the body as a temple in her work and the way she moves through the world. A multi-disciplinary healer and Shamanic facilitator, she says that her spiritual practice is in her work as a teacher and practitioner, an instrument of the Spirit. "I could not do my work if I were not 'a hollow bone'. My life is my faith."

The same need for balance applies to the four yogic paths of Hindu theology – of action (*Karma*), devotion (*Bhakti*), knowledge (*Jnani*), and mysticism (*Raja*). Yoga, really, means union with God; yogis believe that its practice on any path leads to communion with the Divine.

Karma yoga brings together the physical and mental aspects of Hindu philosophy to produce a single concept. Practitioners believe that the present relies on the past and that present actions can alter the future. Steering your actions, including speech and thought, towards the good will facilitate selflessness, eliminate egoistic and negative behaviour, and enable you to influence your destiny.

The term "*bhakti*" can be roughly translated to mean "devotion". Coupled with the Christian concept of faith, it is believed to lead to a state of mind which can be described as being immersed in *bhakti*. This strand of yoga principally advocates love and devotion as the path to *moksha* or liberation.

Raja means "royal" and *raja* yoga is said to be the "king" of yogas. It is the path of yoga which is mainly concerned with meditation. During practice, the yogi sits to observe the mind and to silence floating thoughts. The practice induces a sense of centredness and teaches the self honour and respect.

Jnana means wisdom or discernment and focuses on man's intelligence. Yogis have to have an open mind. A unity of intellect and wisdom will enable them to surpass boundaries and look beyond ideological controversies. *Jnana* is the yoga of knowledge – not knowledge in the intellectual sense, but the knowledge of Brahman and Atman and the realisation of their unity. Where the devotee of God follows the promptings of the heart, the *jnani* uses the powers of the mind to discriminate between the real and the unreal, the permanent and the transitory.

Whatever the entry point, assimilation of all approaches to the Divine is necessary for completeness of understanding. In the West the path of knowledge is perhaps the most superficially accessible. Our education system leads to a facility for acquiring knowledge and a skill in analytical thinking. When I first came to my faith in 1996, my first impulse was to undertake a further degree in theology, specialising in Quakerism as a mystic faith in an interfaith context. And then I wondered why I would take an academic approach to something that exists only through our experience. I needed to leave my cerebral habits behind: it was my heart and my spirit that would serve me now. In the event, the path of knowledge has so far in my journey been the least prominent, and I understand from those more steeped in the Hindu path that that is the way that is the hardest.

The truth is, as the author of *The Cloud of Unknowing* knew, that no life is either completely active or completely contemplative; we are all somewhere on the spectrum between the two extremes. "Love", says Carlos Carretto, "is the synthesis of contemplation and action," and we are all called to different kinds of love in action. "I have known the satisfaction of unrestrained action," he says, "and the joy of contemplative life in the dazzling peace of the desert, and I repeat again St Augustine's words: 'Love and do as you will' " (24-5). St Teresa is of the same mind: "What does it matter if we serve in one way or another."

Despite the claim that contemplation and action are one, there are still conflicting views of their relationship. Thomas Merton and Thich Nhat Hanh, Trappist and Buddhist monks respectively, say that contemplation is only half the job – that the object of years of practice is to make one more fit for action in the world; that the movement of the Spirit in us is to be enacted among other people. The other viewpoint is that the *vita activa* must precede the *vita contemplativa,* that action is preparation for contemplation, that indeed active periods of life are the dry times, the fallow periods from which contemplation will develop. The truth would seem to be that the two are indissolubly connected: each feeds the other.

Finding the balance on a daily or yearly basis is a common preoccupation. Few people feel that they get it right and in any life there will be phases tilted more one way, then the other. As a close attention to the needs of our body will inform us of the food necessary to our condition, so being open to the needs of our soul will allow subtle shifts to redress the balance.

"By their fruits shall ye know them." The fruits can be in increased quality of "being" – awareness, awakening – or increased doing. The best of all worlds is doing with increased being. That, I believe, is the true fulfilment of our human potential as spiritual beings. Manifesting the spiritual in the world by what we are, what we do. And how we do it.

There is an Andrei Rublev icon of angels representing the Trinity, sitting down but with wings spread: in contemplation but ready for action. Similarly Merton writes of an icon of the Buddha with one hand supporting a begging bowl, indicating acceptance of grace, the other pointing downwards – a passive attitude to heaven and an active attitude to the world.

10. FAITH IN ACTION

The Lord taught me to act faithfully in two ways…inwardly
to God and outwardly to all.

George Fox

*"Work is my religion." It was a startling beginning to a talk about the
relation of faith and action, but what followed was the story of a life
devoted to selfless service. Margaret works full time with adults
with learning difficulties, and travels particularly to India to help
set up training for similar work. Some years ago, she was asked by
the British Council to go out to India to set up services there and
found how inappropriate it would be to duplicate English methods.
Captivated by the children on Howrah station, Kolkata, she set up a
school on the station. Many years on, TRACKS is now run by local
people and encompasses classes for mothers, outings for the
children, and possibilities for work in other parts of the country.
Margaret returns frequently to India and is currently helping to
rebuild one of the schools in Tamil Nadu which was destroyed by the
2005 tsunami. In her "spare time" Margaret has for many years
worked as a volunteer and trustee for a Quaker charity, supporting
street homeless in London. Work fills her life. Now in her sixties, she
finds respite in regular Quaker worship but castigates herself for
spending little time in contemplation. A recent bout of bronchial
pneumonia and a recurrence of hepatitis might persuade her to find
a better balance.*

The call to service

Why are we called to live "in the world"? Largely because for us

God is in the world, and to interact with our fellow human beings is to do God's work. As St James wrote: "What good is it, my Friends, for someone to say he has faith when his actions do nothing to show it?" (James 2:14).

The call to service is fundamental to most faiths. In Christianity, the call is to be among the suffering of the world, the dispossessed. Love is the centre of the Gospel. Christ's second commandment is to love thy neighbour as thyself. And the greatest of "Faith, hope and charity" is charity (love).

In nineteenth-century India, Swami Vivekananda persuaded his brother disciples to give up their peaceful meditation and religious individualism and engage in social service: "Where should you go to seek for God? Are not all the poor, the miserable, the weak, good? Why not worship them first? Why go to dig a well on the shores of the Ganges? Let these people be your God – think of them, work for them, pray for them incessantly. The Lord will show you the way" (quoted in Suda, 130). The primary object of Arya Samaj, a modern branch of Hinduism, is "to do good to the world by improving the physical, spiritual, and social conditions of mankind" (Suda, 123). Its followers have set up orphanages, denounced early marriages, and worked for disaster relief and for the abolition of the caste system.

Followers of Hare Krishna too are devoted to service, for instance providing hot meals for homeless people on the streets of London. Their founder, Swami Prabhupada, quoted the Bhagavad Gita in saying you can "become transcendental to the material conceptions of life... only by devotional service and nothing else ... Only through the process of *bhakti* can one understand God" (13).

For Christians God is love. In Islam, to reduce the disparities between rich and poor is a priority: one of its five pillars is charity. Jains must give to charity anything beyond their own needs. Sufis are expected to have a constructive vocation; and, for Sikhs, Guru Nanak said that "true spiritual life meant the performance of duties in the world, and facing and solving the moral and spiritual problems of mankind" (Suda, 223). Buddhism is unusual in its silence on the topic. A Zen practitioner told me that Zen leads to submission and stoic composure, that it has nothing to say about relationship and how we are in the world. Although compassion is a mainstay of Buddhism, it does not necessarily imply love in action. Nonetheless, there has grown up a division of Buddhism, called "engaged" Buddhism, common to most of its denominations, which is active in the world, and recognises the need for change in the structure outside as well as in the structure within. Despite the fear of political engagement among contemplatives, especially in Thailand, the example of the Vietnamese Zen master, Thich Nhat Hanh, and the insistence of such leaders as the current Dalai Lama, on the importance of social service have gone a long way to promote the importance of relationship with all people and the earth. Western influence too has stimulated an ethos of "social service, of compassion in action (rather than just on the meditation cushion)" (Mackenzie, 187). There is now an international network of engaged Buddhists with a collective structure and shared practice.

Biblically, love means to serve, and it is in service that we find our mission in the world. The universality of this message is reflected in the lives of many I have spoken to. From those in, respectively, the Shamanic and the engaged Buddhist traditions I heard: "You have to be in service" and "It is about living with the sacred in daily life; to practise and to serve."

So is our service in obedience to commandments, or in copying the example of a master? How does our faith translate into action? Great acts of selflessness, service for excluded and destitute people, are carried out every day by those of no faith; what is it that a faithful life brings that is particular? What is the process?

My own experience is of the dynamic nature of the Holy Spirit. The love of God works through us and enables us to mirror that love. And the love of God that we receive is not only direct, but through other people. It is reciprocal, circular. In giving we receive. The concept of "do-goodery" is so mistaken. In working with other human beings: whether homeless people, prisoners, asylum seekers, the marginalised and excluded, it is we who receive. The connection we feel with people living in destitution is at a far more powerful level than usual social interaction. It is as if their lives have stripped away the inessentials, and we are privileged to touch them at that point.

One sub-zero January night a group of us were taking tea and sandwiches to people living on the streets of London. A thin middle-aged woman with bare legs and a cotton dress asked us for a blanket, but we had run out. A young man a few yards away called out to say that she could have his blanket. I said: "But you'll get cold; that's all you've got." He said: "She needs it more than I do. What's life about if you can't give a little love?"

Two people made the point that we should thank people we work with for giving us the opportunity for generosity. In fact one woman I spoke to felt that we should ask forgiveness of the dispossessed for using their pain to move us toward enlightenment. When I came to Friends, after a frustrating lifetime of believing, as I had been told from childhood on, that I could not make a difference to the injustice and poverty I saw around me, I found people who *were* making a difference. Perhaps in small, local ways, but I could see that it was possible for me as for them.

The particularly Quaker connection is, I believe, to do with the do-it-yourself nature of the Society: we have to take responsibility for the practice of our faith, for its structures and its financing – there is no paid minister to do it for us. This in turn leads many not to rely on politicians or "experts" but to take personal responsibility for what is happening in the world: "If not me, then who?" It is too because of a strong belief in the power of the Spirit, so available to us in worship, that we trust that Spirit in our fellows, to be able to make a difference. It was someone's leap of faith to enable another without the "relevant" experience to embark on a new life of social activity that changed my life, and has continued to do so. My frequent misgivings about "the difference" any work I do can make to the world are tempered by Mother Teresa's words: "To God there is nothing small. The moment we have given it to God, it becomes infinite." The more I am involved in the voluntary sector, the more I see of people of all faiths and none who give of themselves, who are making a difference, are taking responsibility.

Quakers were involved in the early days of the abolition of the slave trade and prison reform, in the founding of charities such as Amnesty International and Oxfam and, as pacifists, they have been at the forefront of conscientious objection. It is not accidental that Quakers hold to testimonies rather than a creed, for they view faith and action as different facets of the same thing.

The word "testimony" is used by the Quakers to describe a witness to the living truth within the human heart as it is acted out in everyday life. It is not a form of words, but a mode of life based on the realisation that there is that of God in everybody, that all human beings are equal, that all life is interconnected.

Harvey Gillman in *Quaker Faith & Practice*: 23.12

It is not that action is the result of faith; each feeds the other. Even if the work is begun in a far from spiritual frame of mind – grumpy, unwilling – the feelings catch up with the action.

As Jonathan Dale, commenting on the previous passage, says: "Faith, spirituality, God, our sense of the ultimate – however we refer to it – is not a separate place or activity, some secret garden apart from our everyday world. It is experienced in every context of our lives. The 'living truth' longs to be embodied in all that we are and say and do" (Dale, 19). These passages express a central truth for people living a committed life in the world. Justice is a material expression of faith, not an abstraction.

Robert Kennedy reminded us that social forces are made up of the commitments of individuals:

Let no one be discouraged by the belief that there is nothing one man or one woman can do against the enormous array of the world's ills – against misery and ignorance, injustice and violence...Few will have the greatness to bend history itself; but each of us can work to change a small portion of events, and in the total of all those acts will be written the history of this generation...

It is from the numberless diverse acts of courage and belief that human history is shaped. Each time a man stands up for an ideal, or acts to improve the lot of others, or strikes out against injustice, he sends a tiny ripple of hope, and crossing each other from a million different centres of energy and daring, those ripples build a current which can sweep down the mightiest walls of oppression and resistance.

Gandhi was the ultimate *karmayogi*. Part of his greatness was his contribution in making religion practical, a matter of daily and hourly life; hard labour at the heart of life. "God", he once said, "can only appear to the poorest of the poor in the form of *work*" (Chatterjee, 92).

Gandhi...sees this dilemma much as men of faith and conscience in other parts of the world see it today – how to be of service in the world while at the same time sensitive to those outreachings of the spirit which seems to beckon us further still...He once said that meditation and worship were not exclusive things to be kept locked up in a strong box. They must be seen in every act of ours.

ibid.,11

Kshama, a devout Hindu, runs the Chinmaya Tapovan Trust, a large NGO in north-west India. For her and the hundreds who work for her, worship is service, contemplation is in action. All work in all the projects starts with prayer and with devotional ritual to their founder, Guru Dev.

Two of the Anglican priests that I interviewed exemplify the extreme active engagement end of the spectrum. Terry is a prison chaplain, and his work governs his life. He works with prisoners, trying to help them come to terms not only with their criminal activities and their addictions, but the pain that often underlies them, in order to enable men to move on and get a life beyond a constant cycle of re-offending. The stories of abuse, both physical and sexual, or of a parent's suicide, emerge after hours of patient listening and some tough talk. He gives his mobile phone number to partners, children, parents of prisoners, often keeping in touch with the men themselves after they leave. Central to Terry's life and work is his love for these less obviously loveable members of humanity. That love is apparent, as is theirs for him. His only time for reflection is the drive to work, or an occasional afternoon off, walking across the fields.

Peter is also stretched to the limit in his four parishes, and finds little time for contemplation.

All I tend to do is work, but when you stop you realise it's never-ending. I should be visiting, consoling, planning, praying. There is no end to it, there is no natural lull; you could do sixteen hours a day every day of the week and because it's haphazard, reactive, you could immerse yourself in it, lose yourself. Perhaps that is what we should be doing.

Owen Jones, 152

Making a living

Money is needed to live in the world, to raise families: how people manage to integrate that into their spiritual lives, how they bring their faith to bear on their work, how their work expresses their faith, calls for tough discernment. Adhering to the Buddhist precept of "Right Livelihood" can be hard. Not all are able to make a living in something that is fulfilling and expresses their authenticity. Like artists, some work part-time in order to spend the rest of their time in more rewarding activities; some see their call to reform institutions from within; others manage on very little in order to work in an area that they feel called to. At different times of life, different decisions will be made.

In most traditions there is a recognition of the needs of the different stages of life. In Native American cultures, there are important rites to mark the passing from one stage to another. At birth, puberty, marriage and death, people are considered to be particularly close to the spirit world: it is a time of vulnerability and potential. The Hindus have clear-cut divisions between each stage of life: first comes *Brahmachariya*: a period of training of mind and body; then *Grihastha*: the householder period; then, at about the age of 50, *Vanprastha*: retreating from the world with a partner, if wanted, and handing over responsibilities to children; and finally *Sanyas*: time to let go and work towards becoming a liberated soul and the mystic union with the Divine. In Western cultures a similar pattern may emerge. Jung recognised the changing priorities of the second half of life, and the increased urgency of a search for meaning. After a period of education and training in youth, there is often a period of career busyness and building up a home, before a possible stage of retreat, increased interiority and simplification of life. The different stages of life still have their expression in enclosed communities: there will be a time to be trained, for taking responsibility, for teaching, for letting go. This is a generalisation, of course, and many of the people interviewed in this book have not followed the cultural norm. Some people in their twenties and thirties have already found their path, and have made decisions about work accordingly. Dani knew in her teens what her life would be as a celibate Catholic, and has lived it consistently ever since. Mike went into youth work early on. After an early religious experience, he didn't want to work for money but just to help. After training as a teacher, he chose to work with difficult adolescents, "both to ease their discomfort and the discomfort they caused everyone else". Mirabai, now in her thirties, is a learning mentor in a tough local London school. She feels education, being with children, is central to her calling. She teaches yoga to small children, and wants to teach peace education in schools. At lunch-time she sits in meditation with a candle and sometimes a few children join her. For many of the people I talked to the primary focus of early years was a struggle to find a spiritual home, and their working lives reflected that. Earning a living was a secondary priority.

Certain professions are more or less completely incompatible with the achievement of man's final end; and there are certain ways of making a living which do so much physical and, above all, so much moral, intellectual and spiritual harm that, even if they could be practised in a non-attached spirit (which is generally impossible), they would still have to be eschewed by anyone dedicated to the task of liberating, not only himself, but others.

Huxley, 137

Huxley is talking not only about criminal activities but about activities to which people might have a conscientious objection: the manufacture of arms, the army for Quakers, butchery for vegetarians, usury for Muslims and in the past for Christians. In many occupations, as he indicates, it takes a good deal of detachment to be true to a spiritual life, but it is important to many I have spoken to not to divorce themselves from the nitty gritty. Recognising that we are in the world means not separating ourselves from the tensions of working with other people or the dilemmas of working, for instance, in the corporate or political sector. Choices have to be made as to whether to work on, for instance, a defence contract, or on the advertising account of a cigarette manufacturer. Continual discernment is called for. Priha, a Jain, works as an investment banker in the City of London. I asked if it was not difficult to practise her faith in such an environment. "Oh no," she replied. "It is difficult to practise the faith but I feel it is important to have awareness of one's purpose in life – getting as close as possible if not actually attaining *moksha* in this lifetime. So, at work I need to have reminders to keep me aware of my purpose: for example when I walk to the drinks machine, I try to meditate (my interpretation is being in a peaceful state of mind)."

St Francis wrote in his Rule that people should as far as possible use their skills, and work in their original occupations "if it is not harmful to their soul's salvation and if it is convenient to do so". The people I interviewed work in a wide range of jobs: catering, acting, hairdressing, dance, gardening and librarianship. Three run or have run NGOs; some run retreats; a number are teachers, of small children, of adults with learning difficulties, of

English in a foreign land. Several are healers or counsellors; others are retired or work sporadically, many as volunteers – in peace-making, homelessness, prisons, with severely disabled children or at risk families – to maintain their spiritual lives. The distinction between work and leisure, work and holidays, paid and voluntary work, is often blurred. For those whose lives are of a piece, such distinctions have little meaning. Work is a natural expression of their true selves.

Ways of working

Work is also a connection with others. There is an inter-relation in work as in the rest of our lives. On an intimate scale, evident in the sharing of well-being between a Reiki healer and her patient, the flowing of energy from one to another, it is also present in wider networks – with our clients, customers, those we serve, those we work with, those from whom we get the raw materials – all is intertwined. Many are struggling to get a better balance in what they do. A spiritual and holistic healer in Louisiana whose "work and practice are reflected in every action I take throughout the day", expressed dissatisfaction. The context of her work was not all she wanted it to be; she wanted to give more to her community and perhaps work in prison. She wanted the ripples of her work to have an effect in the world. A year later, the New Orleans floods gave her the opportunity. As she led groups of therapists and healers in round-the-clock shifts, treating the rescue workers and police, her prayers were answered. She has now been appointed the Louisiana State Coordinator of the Emergency Response Massage International organization, focusing on "the support of the first responders in times of catastrophic events".

One welcome recognition of the interplay between faith and action is The Center for Action and Contemplation. Located in Albuquerque, New Mexico, it was founded in 1987 by Franciscan Father Richard Rohr. Father Rohr saw the need for a training/formation centre that would serve as a place of discernment and growth for activists and those interested in social service ministries. There they would come, be still, and learn how to integrate a contemplative lifestyle and compassionate service. They would live a social spirituality. This centre would serve a dual purpose as not only a radical voice for peaceful, non-violent social change but also as a forum for renewal and encouragement for the seeking individual who sought direction from and understanding of God's will and love. Among their beliefs are: "Prayer and involvement with the issues of our time; a simple non-violent life, rooted in the Gospels; and living and promoting the call to lay leadership". Their commitment is to engage actively in transforming society from a faith perspective.

It is not only what we do but, more importantly, how we do it. Mike has lived most of his life in running charitable organisations and starting up innovative projects. His management style is unorthodox, relying on the guidance of synchronicity, seeming coincidence – a phone call, a piece on the radio – that confirms a course of action. He rejects the false division between contemplation and action. "What has to happen is that you be what you are doing," and gave me a little poem:

Do be do be do
Take more time to be
and spend less on the do,
they said, as if these are alternatives

like in do-be-do-be-do,

but I think they're better inter-twined

spirit enacted, action inspired,

so in future I'll strive to de,

or perhaps it should be "boo"!

"Right Action" is of course part of the Buddhist eight-fold path. Peter, a Buddhist Quaker, prefers the term "benevolent action", which signifies an outward as well as an inner motion. He defines it as an outward journey arising from an inner one. Steindl-Rast talks of "Aligning your work with your best intentions" (5), a good way of describing an approach to the complexities of life's demands. Such an approach may be less goal-driven than the usual ways of the world and with less attachment to the outcome. A woman who runs an ecumenical community centre gave an example of making an Spirit-based choice:

> When we employ companies/contractors to work for us, we try to go for small, local businesses to whom the job will make a difference rather than supporting big conglomerates (for the cleaning we had a choice between a couple sponsored by the Prince's Trust and a US Conglomerate – the couple got it!) There's something here re the priority of the individual over cold, naked finances and profit.

The motivation is key: decisions will be made not through expedience but because it is the right thing to do. Love in action is our aspiration, and there are different ways of expressing it.

That expression, of course, is not only in grand works of social action but in the small doings of our everyday life: in the way we relate to our partners, our children, our parents. Loving acts are to be seen every moment of the day, even in the stress-filled centres of big cities. On the bus, a young mother gives up her seat for an elderly Muslim man; a man on a bike chases after a woman whose hat has blown off in the wind. Despite all news reports to the contrary, kindness is alive and well in modern life. It is for us to be alive to the opportunities. To be mindful, not so taken up with our own preoccupations, worries and plans that we fail to notice the old woman trying to cross the road. Not in such a rush that we haven't the patience to listen to a tourist with bad English telling us he is lost. Seeing two women warmly greeting each other in the street, I thought how random our acquaintance is. Just because we have met before, we greet a passer-by, have a conversation. Why not greet the people behind her? A smile, a greeting to the street cleaner, the news vendor, the postman; thanks to a motorist who waits for us to cross the road – small courtesies make a difference. We do not know what a difficult day someone else is having, the effect our smallest action can have. As we will know from our own experience, a warm response from a stranger when we were feeling low can produce a lasting glow – and yet it was probably barely noticed by the person who gave it, and immediately forgotten.

Be patterns, be examples in all countries, places, islands, nations, wherever you come, that your carriage and life may preach among all sorts of people, and to them; then you will come to walk cheerfully over the world, greeting that of God in everyone.

George Fox

11. OBEDIENCE: FAITHFULNESS

Most forms of traditional Christian and Buddhist monasticism include requirements to observe obedience, poverty and chastity. In Hindu asceticism too adherence to these observances are generally expected. But what do these vows mean for the committed person living in the world?

The very word "obedience", resonant as it is of school, pointless rules, bossiness, hierarchy, is often enough to turn people away from any positive view of the monastic life. As one Benedictine monk wrote: "To vow oneself for life to what is known as a 'total institution', in which obedience pervades the whole of existence, seems to many people an abdication of human dignity and therefore abhorrent" (Boulding, 134). Certainly I was appalled to read, some years ago, in *Through the Narrow Gate*, of a highly intelligent novice nun being ordered to scrub the steps with a pink nylon nail brush:

> We were being trained in Ignatian obedience, which aims to break down the will and judgement of a religious so that he unquestionably accepts the will of God as it is presented to him through his superior...The superior represents God to a religious: his commands, orders, "the least sign of his will", as the Rule says, are to be taken as a direct message from God.
> Could I really believe that the Infinite Being could think of nothing better than nail brushes?
>
> *Armstrong, 155, 158*

Such behaviour shows the "serious danger of monastic obedience being used ... to frustrate the true purpose of monastic life" (Merton, 1995:15). There are other dangers: Abhishiktananda wrote that he needed years to free himself from the infantilism and the lack of a personal responsibility instilled in him on the pretext of obedience. Indeed, he wondered if he had actually freed himself. Within a monastic community obedience may be to an abbot or Mother Superior, a human representative of God's will, often a receptacle of spiritual wisdom rather than of the abuse of Karen Armstrong's experience. For St Francis and his followers obedience was to each other, the band of brothers, not just to the leader of the order. In the world, to what or whom will such obedience be? For some it will be to the guru who stands in much the same position as the abbot, a human being to whom total obedience is due as part of the discipline essential to progress on the spiritual path. For those living in a community it may be to the communal rule, the communal good, an ethical position to which all in the community have agreed. For all – and centrally for those trying to live their faith in the world – it will be obedience to God, to the Spirit, the inner voice, the better self, the intuition that guides us on our way.

An interior process

Western education trains us to use our minds in logic and analytical reasoning. Being present to God is a different kind of discipline: an opening of the heart, a listening to what can be intuitively known, rather than to what can be rationally deduced. In being obedient we have to choose to put first insights of the heart rather than to batter the universe with demands to have our questions answered. In our imperfect human state we have to learn to live with unanswered questions.

For obedience is far beyond just following the rules. It is an interior process, not an imposition, and its manifestations are not necessarily visible. The eleventh-century Sufi, Sheikh Abdullah Ansari, dismisses age-old traditions of outward show: "Fasting is only the saving of bread. Formal prayer is for old men and women. Pilgrimage is a worldly pleasure. Conquer the heart – its mastery conquest indeed" (quoted in Stuart, 360).

For me, obedience means trust, is the very meaning of "faith", the surrender of ambition, plans, decisions made by the ego and the urge to control. Some may feel that their freedom is being curbed, but by freeing ourselves from slavery to our impulses we are gaining a far greater freedom. We need to admit how little we know of the larger scheme of things, to be content in our unknowingness, "listening ever to Eternity's whisper, walking with a smile into the dark" (Kelly, 74). "Thy will be done" is for me the only prayer of any worth. It will "be done" whether we pray for it or not, but our prayer aligns us with that purpose, marks our acceptance. Obedience to that will, however we discern it, is life's major task, allowing God to work in us. "Obedience" now is for me a fundamental, perhaps the central, part of the sacramental life. With the world inside as our guide, we have moments of choice: to betray our true self or to say "yes".

In 1939 Thomas Kelly gave the annual William Penn lecture on "Holy Obedience". He identifies a formidable task. Quoting Meister Eckhart, he says:

"There are plenty to follow our Lord half-way, but not the other half. They will give up possessions, friends and honors, but it touches them too closely to disown themselves." It is just this astonishing life which is willing to follow Him the other half, sincerely to disown itself, this life which intends *complete* obedience, without *any* reservations which I would propose to you in all humility, in all boldness, in all seriousness...When such a commitment comes in a human life, God breaks through, miracles are wrought, world-renewing divine forces are released, history changes.

(52)

Impassioned, inspiring – and so daunting! But Kelly goes on to analyse the task in a practical way. There are, he says, four gateways to obedience. First comes the call, the experience that asks it of us. Secondly, he says, "Begin where you are. Obey *now*. Use what little obedience you are capable of, even if it be like a grain of mustard seed"; thirdly "If you slip and stumble and forget God for an hour, and assert your old proud self, and rely upon your own clever wisdom, don't spend too much time in anguished regrets and self-accusations but begin again, just where you are." And, finally, "Learn to live in the passive voice...and let life be willed through you. For 'I will' spells not obedience" (60-61).

It was only ten years ago that I began to understand about learning to live in the passive voice, learning to let go of my own willing. It was not a cerebral understanding, but an understanding reached, as in most spiritual development, in the act itself. Realising that I needed to give up the career of some thirty years, and with considerable preparation to safeguard my clients, I sold my business. I had no idea of what I would do, *and it didn't matter*. The necessity that impelled me and the freedom that awaited me combined to make it the most powerful spiritual experience of my life so far. Why had it taken me so long to understand that this was the way to live my life? How had I not realised the enormous relief of surrendering my will to make things happen, and resting in the faith that it would be shown? It *has* been shown and continues to be so. As with all lessons in life, it is an ongoing one. The urge to let go continues to make itself felt in all parts of life, as and when we are ready.

Discernment

Of course discernment is not easy. Patience is an essential attribute, and one with which many of us struggle. The Spirit's time is not ours. Only by waiting and accepting that what is right will be shown at its proper time can we be true to the process. We alone cannot make things happen; believing that we can only leads to frustration. Pink Dandelion talks of early Quakers' "continual struggle to discern what might be the obedient path"; for those who seek faithfulness, the struggle continues. Barry and Connolly describe discernment at its basic level as consisting of recognising differences. One of the criteria that people use to decide whether an experience is of God is to compare it with another experience, a touchstone experience, that they know is of God. Another helpful pointer that a friend gave me was that if a decision is about what you're embracing, that's fine; if it's about avoidance, "it's dodgy".

One test of true discernment in prayer or in action is in the fruits of that action. If prayer leads to joy and inner peace, love and compassion, if action leads to an increase in justice and a better life for others, it may be said to be of God. Barry and Connolly identify another helpful criterion of discernment: "the developing sense of the reality of God as someone who is not within the directee's control". As a friend of mine was told some years ago, "There are two things you need to know about God: firstly, that God exists, and secondly, that it isn't you." Experience needs to lead to humility – not self-abasement, but self-forgetfulness.

For many this is a hard tightrope to walk. The balance between a proper exploitation of our natural talents and an equally proper humility is a constant test of our faithfulness. Hiding our Light under a bushel will benefit no one: "Gifts" is what they are, God-given, and given to be used. But in all needs to be remembered "Not I, but God in me". We are enabled, empowered, literally inspired, to go beyond what seem to be our own capabilities. When the action is right, the way forward will be given, and the competence to follow it. Jan whose practice is principally Buddhist and shamanic, though with many years' attendance at a Quaker Meeting, talks of reaching "a place of integrity". "Integrity", she says, "comes from giving yourself permission to be spontaneous. I love the moment when you know what you have to do but not why. You jump off the cliff, and you fly."

In many traditions discernment is not left up to the individual but relies on the traditions of orthodoxy or entrusted to a wiser, more experienced "master". In other circles such testing is done corporately, mutually, by one's peers, rather than a "superior"; the Quakers have Meetings for Clearness which can be called when an individual feels the need for the supportive wisdom of a group of Friends.

I have already referred to Mike's discernment in relying on synchronicity to guide decision-making in his work as the head of an NGO. For myself too synchronicity plays a major part, a revelation of a previously hidden connection. One man goes so far as to say that he is disappointed when he becomes aware of a synchronicity: the connection has been there all the time, and he has only just become aware of it. For God is connection, relationship, the linking factor in all living beings. When we act according to that connection, reinforcing relationship between people, we are being obedient to God's will.

It is in little things, I increasingly realise, that our obedience, or faithfulness – a softer word, with intimations of continuity and relationship, as well as the inclusion of "faith" – is most often tested. When shopping, I struggle with my meanness in paying more for organic goods; in a hurry, do I push forward in a busy street or care for the others in my way? Do I listen with love to another's point of view, or do I thrust forward my own? In the Rule of the Iona Community, the task in hand "mainly consists of small mundane things which are hard to feel very spiritual about, and which at times seem utterly relentless". Ruth Burrows says: "I have come to attach great importance to the surrender of self-will in small matters when no principle is involved, but it is only a question of another's will confronting mine" (Burrows, 93). "Every tiny decision, taken in the light," says Jonathan Dale, "reclaims the world of secular, routine practices, for God" (68-9).

Even, or perhaps especially, the difficulties in our life have significance, if only in hindsight. I have been burgled a number of times. I inherited some beautiful Victorian jewellery from my grandmother, and was given other lovely things by my husband. Again and again, lovely things were taken from me, until most of them were simply a memory, and I could not remember what I actually still possessed. It gradually ceased to matter, and I realised the other day that the forcible "letting go" of those possessions was a signpost to my later joyous relinquishing of much of the rest.

Transforming power

Perhaps it is in our response to suffering that we are most tested in our faithfulness. Pain and loss are inherent in the human condition; there are areas of great hurt in us all that we do not care to revisit too often. Acceptance of suffering is at the heart of Buddhism; the cross the central symbol in Christianity. Jan who has had ongoing health problems for some years reached an understanding that perhaps she didn't need to be well – it has not stopped her in her work in mediation and conflict resolution – leading business courses on "dealing with difficult customers", entering, as she says, a room full of angry men. There are, she said, opportunities in every situation. "Everything is perfect. Where is the perfection in this moment?"

For most of us, though, and for most of the time, the acceptance of suffering feels beyond us. Even if we have seen in hindsight how we have been deepened, our humility and understanding of others increased, by times of grief or illness; even if we manage intellectually to accept its potential for our spiritual development, in our hearts we cry out: "Why this? Why me?"

A description of suffering as being squeezed so closely by God that we can barely breathe is perhaps intellectually helpful, but few of us can embrace suffering with the degree of eagerness of those who ask for it, in order to move forward in their quest, or the acceptance expressed by an elderly member of my Meeting after the death of her life-long partner: "I want to thank God for everything, including the things I didn't want."

The Dalai Lama refers to the Chinese who occupy his country as "my friends, the enemy", saying that they have been his greatest teachers. A friend described the invasion of Tibet as having brought a "Tibetan invasion": only since their country was overrun have the Tibetans given their spiritual wisdom to the world.

In the world we define everything in terms of opposites; indeed we can often only understand something in terms of the existence of an opposite: light/dark, good/evil, happiness/suffering. Externalised, this duality can lead to conflict – a natural part of human existence, but it does not have to lead to violence or division. We live in a society with political and criminal justice systems that are polarised and confrontational; we are encouraged to debate, to argue, to take opposite points of view. It does not have to be so. A central concept in the Alternatives to Violence project (AVP), is that of Transforming Power. TP is something we have all known intuitively and experientially. Sometimes, during an argument, if we don't react immediately, if we take time, it allows space into the conflict, a space into which can enter another possibility, a third, or middle way not previously thought of. It is not either this or that, but something else.

The general world-view of duality encourages a blame culture, demonising difference and "the other". The Buddhist belief in the Buddha nature in all and the Quaker equivalent of "that of God in everyone" encourage a non-dualistic view. We are all connected; there is no "other". By blaming, punishing, killing another we are damaging the Spirit in all. The question "What would you do about Hitler?" comes up often in enquirers' gatherings. The Zen priest

Rev. Jiyu-Kennett has an answer:

> If I say that Hitler is difficult to see as a Buddha, I am trying to kill Buddha...Because we cannot recognise the Buddha in all things we constantly kill the Buddha. We can know, we can feel instinctively that Buddha is everywhere but we have not understood...that our bones, flesh, blood, marrow....yes, and our sexual side as well, and all the mud and the things we hate and all the torture side of ourselves and all the evil, all is *the* aspect of the Buddha mind.
>
> (103)

In *Salvaging the Sacred*, Marion Partington writes about her sister who was one of the victims of a mass murderer. She bears witness that *in extremis* we may be driven to recognise that we are all capable both of murder, and of love.

When we can begin to internalise apparent contradictions, to know in our hearts our own capacity for both good and evil, not to project the shadow on to others; when we can understand that it is by holding apparent opposites in tension that we can understand wholeness, then we are approaching *advaita*, a non-dualistic experience of the God within and without. In the silence of our hearts we can encompass all. The Buddha talked of the Middle Way: neither self nor not self.

Merton (1975) writes: "It is really this total and uncompromising docility to the will of God that gives a man a taste for spiritual things. It is this delicate instinct to yield to the slightest movement of God's love that makes the true contemplative. As St Thomas [Aquinas] says: '...It is obedience that makes man fit to see God.'"

12. POVERTY: SIMPLICITY

Gyan refers to himself a renunciate. He is an Englishman in his fifties; a handsome man with shaven head, brilliant blue eyes and a wicked sense of humour. At an early age he decided not to have children. For twelve years he lived as a disciple of Swami Satyananda in an ashram in India: a holy man in saffron robes. He has never owned a house or furniture. He has no pension, no insurance: like the lilies of the field he considers not the morrow, but trusts that all will be given. For the last few years he has lived with his girlfriend in Italy, undertaking the building work to turn an ancient estate into a yoga centre. He works for three weeks a year as chef for a Buddhist retreat of some 400 people in Australia. This enables him to devote himself to retreats in different countries. He recently spent some months on a retreat in Toronto with a master "who gives me a hard time. It is extremely good for me." At the Italian yoga centre chanting is commonplace, as is silent meditation. One night there is a concert; Indian drumming fills the air – hard to believe we are in Italy. On the notice board are images of Mary, the Buddha: Gyan describes himself as a yogi of the Vedantic tradition, who enjoys studying Buddhist philosophy, Christ being his inner heart icon (or Ishtadevata). "I carry my cell with me" he says.

Modern life in developed countries is complicated. The intricacies of housing benefit or tax forms, the increasing sophistication of machines such as computers and mobile phones that did not even exist a century ago, constantly changing fashions in clothes and design style. It is not surprising that more and more people fail to keep up and fall off the edges of our communities. I am thinking of neighbours affected by confusion, by mental illness, those with learning difficulties, those who turn to addiction to cover feelings of inadequacy, those in prison, those without adequate homes, many elderly people who feel that they simply can't cope. I am not advocating a return to the horse and cart (although that would be ecologically attractive), but I am reminded of a scene from the play *Becket* by Jean Anouilh. Thomas à Becket is talking to King Henry II who queries his use of an unfamiliar word: "Forks?"

Becket: Yes. It's a new instrument, a devilish little thing to look at and to use too. It's for pronging meat and carrying it to your mouth. It saves you dirtying your fingers.
King: But you dirty the fork?
Becket: Yes, but it's washable.
King: So are your fingers. I don't see the point.

(10)

Travelling in countries where traffic lights are an innovation, attending a workshop on a Pacific island about the introduction and co-operative ownership of electricity, sitting on the ground eating with my right hand off a banana leaf, I wonder why we have so complicated our lives. One day I realised that I had not seen a mirror for several months, and thought what a difference that had made to my daily life: less concern with how I looked, what I was wearing, less self-consciousness, more concentration, perhaps, on less superficial matters. Most of all, I had not been aware of its absence. Living in the moment, awareness of all that surrounds us, includes wonder at the ingenuity of man, appreciating the complexities – and taking a long look at what is really necessary in our lives.

Why poverty? Why should we voluntarily seek a state with which large numbers of the world's population struggle on a daily basis? Poverty in its usual sense has little of the spiritual about it: a daily fight for survival is not to be romanticised; too much effort spent on keeping oneself alive does not lend itself to a spiritual view of the world. Although it is true too that those who have least often seem most in touch with their essential selves.

But "poverty" as used in a spiritual context indicates a poverty that has been chosen, freely entered into. Christian monastic tradition has a particular understanding of the word – formally, "effective poverty" – that means a relinquishing of all one's worldly goods to the religious community, and to God, divesting oneself of all money and personal possessions. For Benedictines poverty is renunciation and detachment. In general, that is not to go without; the community looks after its own, and in old age community members are cared for, and a burial paid for. Nearer to "real" poverty is the life of the mendicant or *sannyasi*, who in old age leaves home and possessions behind and travels with a begging bowl, committing himself to a life of insecurity and dependence on others for alms. Even then the wider community in India takes responsibility for its *sannyasi*, seeing it as a duty to feed those whose role is seen as an important contribution to the world at large. Much as I admire those who live such a life, when I saw the queue of people for the daily free meal outside one ashram in India, I felt keener to give to those whose poverty was unchosen than to those who stood beside them in their saffron robes.

What is the point of voluntary "poverty"? Perhaps "simplicity" is a better word: less an affront to those whose poverty is not chosen, and more indicative of a mode of life in its totality. Buddha relinquished his wealth and embraced a life of noble poverty; Jesus said: "How hardly shall they that have riches enter into the kingdom of God". People as diverse as Confucius, Lao-Tzu, Mohammed, Thoreau and Gandhi have paid tribute to the value of simplicity; it is widely felt among those on a spiritual path that preoccupation with the material world is a barrier to a spiritual life.

Removing the clutter

My own favourite definition of simplicity is "removing the clutter" between oneself and God. For Quakers such "clutter" includes the rituals and externals of religious services; their practice is stripped down, utterly simple in its lack of set words, dogma, anything that might interfere with the relationship between the Meeting and God. Meetings can take place at any time and in any place – no building is more sacred than another – and meeting houses themselves are bare of symbols and ornamentation. In reform Islam too there has been a stripping down of the accretions of ritual and superstition accrued over the centuries.

Simplicity in our daily life is a compassionate approach to the world, an expression of our interconnectedness. It is in our relationships with other people and the rest of the created world that God is expressed, so removing clutter that creates a barrier in that relationship is also a fundamental part of simplicity. An increasing imperative is to leave a light footprint on the earth; such simplicity is defined by not using up too many of the earth's resources, for the sake of mankind and the earth. Using alternative sources of energy, lowering levels of personal consumption, using products that are non-polluting, durable and easy to repair, living without a car, trying not to travel by plane, shopping for natural food and items that have not consumed too much energy in their transportation.

The Lifestyle Movement is an organisation dedicated to these issues, working, it says, to provide inspiration and practical advice to people who aspire to live in a way that reflects the ideal of justice for the earth and for those who live on it. It combines a position on personal lifestyle with active support of groups working for environmental, developmental and peace issues. It seeks to inform its members on issues such as globalisation, international debt, resource use, genetically-modified organisms, political exploitation and social justice and to point to the (often complex) connections between these issues.

Our way of life will not be static but a growing awareness and response to changing conditions. Jonathan Dale talks of "going beyond the comfort zone" in the wrestling with our daily choices in travel, housing and shopping. And wrestling it is. "How far is enough? Should we feel virtuous for being a vegetarian or guilty for not being a vegan? Is it good to trade in a BMW for a mini, or should we be cycling to the station? Such questions arise continuously, yet there can be no straightforward answer" (quoted in Dale, 23).

When I gave up my car many years ago, it was for economic rather than green reasons. At first it seemed impossible: we were so reliant on the car to take the children to their activities. Some adjustments had to be made – we moved to a nearer nursery, a different piano teacher – and then a car-free existence became not only possible but pleasurable. For people living without adequate public transport, that may not be an option, but our choices are often wider than we at first realise.

Alongside the poor

Some people divest themselves of many of their possessions, living simply in order to live alongside the poor, to put themselves on a level with those who have least, in a spirit both of equality and the message of the Sermon on the Mount. Thich Nhat Hanh is quoted as saying: "Do not accumulate wealth while millions are hungry... Live simply and share time, energy, and material resources with those who are in need." Fasting for part of the day as is the practice in many Buddhist monasteries can be seen as part of a solidarity with those in need. As Gandhi said: "Live simply that others may simply live." Carol Carretto, writing from the point of view of a Little Brother of Jesus, writes: "If I love, if I really love, how can I tolerate the fact that a third of humanity is menaced by starvation while I enjoy the security of economic stability?" The Little Brothers live in community with the poorest, a desert in the city.

But not all will be in agreement. The Dutch priest, Henri Nouwen, raises a crucial question about living an authentic life: "Can we truly live with the poor?...Some say yes, some say no. Some say that to be a priest for the poor, you should be no different from them, others say that it is not realistic or even authentic" (in Durback, 137-8). Each will answer according to his or her inner truth.

Spareness

For myself, removing the clutter has taken the form of ridding myself of many of my possessions. After a year's travelling I found, somewhat to my surprise, that I did not want my flat, did not want the handsome but rather formal furniture from my marriage or that I had inherited. The trappings of that middle-class life no longer represented the me I had become. More than that, it seemed important to divest myself not only of material objects, but of the constant distraction that they represented: each a reminder of someone or something, drawing me into other worlds.

When my mother came to visit the other day, she commented that I had nothing on the walls. "Why not?" she asked.

"I don't want to be distracted."

"Oh," said my mother, "you have changed."

And I have. The blankness of the walls suits me well, a reminder of the space of the inner and outer desert which has had such a powerful influence on me. Spareness is a vehicle for mindfulness; it concentrates the mind on the present moment and on what there is. In a prison, a patch of blue sky is precious; in the desert the tracery of the trail of a single black beetle captures the heart; a single tree in the middle of the city can be more treasured than a whole orchard in rural surroundings. Quality supersedes quantity.

As Steindl-Rast points out, one of the blessings of simplicity is that any addition feels like riches. In a large pot of expectation, a pint will feel little; in a half-pint measure, it will be full to overflowing. So, if we have ten pairs of earrings, another pair is not of much significance. If we own just one sari, another is luxury indeed. In seeking for more and more, we fail to understand this simple truth, this truth about simplicity.

When I recently had an invasion of "stuff" held in storage to see if I would want it again, I found myself disabled by it, my mind as well as my physical space cluttered. Having done without it for nearly two years, I knew what I wanted, and that the rest could go. Interestingly what I did want – my CDs, to which I was arguably most attached – did not appear. They turned up much later, but the lesson had been learned.

Shedding, once started, is a continuing activity, and the freedom is a delight. No worry about insurance or loss, less paperwork, less preoccupation with upkeep and security, with something that in the final analysis simply doesn't matter; I don't need things to remind me of people that I love. I recognise that I am free to make such a choice; my children are grown; I live alone. At other stages of life it can be more complicated.

It is not just in order to share the poverty of others that we might be drawn to a simpler way of life. It might be in recognition that simpler ways of life practised by people without much choice are actually better, and that most of what we possess we could happily do without. At a recent session of Quaker outreach, one woman said she had been thinking about what she needed to survive. From a scrap of paper she read out the following list:

clean water
enough food
medicines for when I am sick
a roof over my head
some basic clothing
some paper and a pencil - and
(she said)
I do like my TV.

Thinking of those who have less, she said what a lot that was; everyone else in the room was thinking: my goodness, that wouldn't be enough for me.

For Karol, a Canadian living and teaching in Thailand, it was crucial that she lived and worked in the same conditions as her Thai colleagues. She speaks of her own previous life on a large estate in Canada and how she used to be content to "do good" then go home to her comfortable middle-class existence. I know that when I was working in a poor Bangladeshi community in the East End of London I felt a discomfort in returning to my own comfortable flat. It is in listening to that discomfort that we make changes in our lives.

There is a story about William Penn, an early Quaker and founder of the state of Pennsylvania. Part of his apparel as an aristocrat was to wear a sword. He asked George Fox, one of the early members of the Religious Society of Friends (Quakers), whether it was all right to wear one. Fox's response was not "Take it off this instant; we are a pacifist organisation" but "Wear it as long as you can." I find that a good rule to live by: eat meat for as long as you can, buy Nescafé for as long as you can, drink alcohol for as long as you can; give up when and if the discomfort grows too much. Pay attention to the inner truth. We speak of having choices and, of course, compared to those who struggle to survive, we do. But to talk of making decisions is to speak from an external perspective. There is an interior imperative, and the way becomes clear.

Reaching that place of clarity can be painfully slow. Jonathan Dale writes well about the "nagging" process.

Of course it wasn't my family that was nagging me, nor my

friends...It was something else. It was quietly there again and again and again – part of the very fabric of our lives. It never let me go. It wasn't threatening. It wasn't paralysing. It wasn't a command. It was an inner conversation which always ended with my being shown how my lifestyle was inconsistent with my professed beliefs. It was infinitely patient and quietly persuasive. It was the Light in spoken form and it nagged me lovingly into something which I knew in my heart of hearts that I wanted to do, however long my resistance.

(75-6)

One Anglican priest I spoke to said that when his children were grown up, he intended to live rough. I asked if that was to live alongside the poor. He said, "No, it is to live without anything."

"Will you beg?"

"Maybe, or perhaps wash the dishes to pay for a meal."

This is a key issue. For me it would feel a self-indulgence to give up the wherewithall for living and become reliant on others, and I said so. He asked if that was pride or an unwillingness to receive. I said that I thought there were plenty who needed to receive and I didn't need to add to them. Though I am influenced by the *sannyasi* way and would like to reduce my possessions to what I can carry, my "poverty" stops short – or that is how it seems to me now – of making myself dependent on others.

Non-attachment

For some it is "affective poverty" (being indifferent to money) that is more important than how much they actually own. For the community on Iona the emphasis is on equality and detachment:

We follow an economic model which is based on need. Everyone receives an allowance which is the same regardless of job – qualifications, professional standing, age or experience...This poverty is not one of hardship. Rather it is one of simplicity, and of corporate responsibility for money...sharing limited space and material resources...sharing responsibility for appropriate budgeting, all tend towards detachment from material possessions and towards an appreciation of those things that cannot be bought with money.

Members living away from the island give a tenth of their income to the community (for charity and the common fund) and discuss their use of the other 90%.

A Franciscan tertiary expressed a view that poverty is about letting go, being free from attachment while owning things. He feels that St Francis was hung up on poverty as an end in itself, "as if poverty were his bride".

Warren tells the story of a man seeking a spiritual master. In the town he finds a great teacher living in a fine house, surrounded by possessions, and turns away in disgust. Coming to a desert he finds a man in rags sitting on a rock, who clearly must be a master.

He said, "The first teacher I went to was surrounded with possessions. He could not possibly be holy."

The hermit began to weep.

"Why are you crying?" the seeker asked in astonishment.

"That teacher has possessions because he is detached; I couldn't handle such riches, which is why I am here to learn about having nothing."

Krishnamurti says, "We are the things we possess, we are that to which we are attached." Non-attachment is a concept central to many Eastern religions, a concept that goes way beyond material possessions. Letting go of ambition, attachment to the fruits of labour – success or failure; letting go of the need to be well thought of – belongings of another kind, these are harder lessons to learn.

Time

An aspect of simplicity that is central to the concerns of this book is in the use of time, which Pink Dandelion calls "a significant aspect of consumer culture" (8). Busyness can blind us to the workings of the Spirit. We need to free ourselves of preoccupations, clear a space in our minds and hearts, as well as in our living rooms. That applies to all purposeful activity, whether in the home or at work, voluntary action, as well as money-making activities. "The spiritual issue is not whether or not we are busy but whether the use of our time is in the hands of our self or the Godself within" (Dale, 48).

There has to be time to be still, to allow our consciousness to expand beyond the concerns of the everyday, the pressing of clock-related activities, time for timelessness to take over, for intuition to let its voice be heard. When I can, I take my watch off to take "time" out of the equation, let the natural instincts of hunger, awareness of dawn and dusk, take precedence. In Native American cultures the passage of time is viewed as not linear but circular, part of the cyclic nature of the seasons, the rising and setting of the sun, the birth, growth, maturing and death of all creation: plants, animals and people. Being in touch with that motion of time is to be part of the interconnectedness of all creation.

In a working life and within the family, creative ways may have to be found to enable solitude. A less active social life, fewer house guests, making mental space a priority. Collect ourselves, pay attention, be mindful. If prayer is attention, and life is for prayer, then it behoves us to remove as many barriers as we can to paying that full attention. Distance ourselves from the "and then, and then" of our hectic lives, the plans of an ego-driven life, the racing mind so hard to dissolve in meditation, to stillness of the heart. Stop!

Paradoxical as it may seem, the purposeful life has no content, no point. It hurries on and on, and misses everything. Not hurrying, the purposeless life misses nothing, for it is only when there is no goal and no rush that the human senses are fully open to receive the world. Absence of hurry also involves a certain lack of interference with the natural course of events, especially when it is felt that the natural course follows principles which are not foreign to human intelligence. For...the Taoist mentality makes, or forces, nothing but "grows" everything.

Alan Watts in Vardey, 39 8

A simple life

A man disabled in a car crash spoke on the radio of how he welcomed his disability as it made even little things an adventure. Richard Branson, he said, had to go up in a balloon to find his adventure – he himself could find it by crossing the road. Perhaps one of the drives towards simplicity is to find adventure in the everyday, to be closer to the adventure of living.

A simple way of life is no kind of mortification or deprivation: indeed, it can lead to a release of joy. Whether in worship or daily life, external simplicity is an outer expression of an inner freedom, a detachment. Simplicity in outer things allows us to order our inner life, and, as we become more attuned to our inner life, a simplification of externals, less "clutter", may become not a duty nor an expression of social or political views, but a mystic necessity.

To attach a moral dimension to simplicity is to misunderstand; indeed Krishnamurti warns us against finding pleasure "in the pride and vanity of renunciation" (March 9). Guilt about possessions, competitiveness about how little, as well as how much, we own, are dangerous and miss the point.

For those who have choices about how to live, a wide variety of expressions of that inner necessity will be found:

• Two of the people I talked to have decided not to have children, feeling that they would be a complication that would distract them from what they feel called to do.

• An elderly couple living in the Coromandel peninsular of New Zealand live off the grid, using solar and wind energy to power a small fridge, and occasionally a sewing machine.

• A Quaker couple have felt called to live in a poor council estate in the North of England and send their children to the local school, in solidarity with the lives of people who have little choice.

• Kamla, a non-practising Hindu in her early seventies, died in 2006. She was a mathematician who studied and taught at many prestigious schools in England and India. For many years, she devoted herself to running a charity school in a village about 100 miles outside Delhi, living in a scruffy village house far below her previous standard of living.

• Stephen, an Englishman in his sixties who lives in Madagascar, spent 17 years with his Malagasy wife in a village without electricity and in rough weather an eight-hour walk to the nearest neighbour. He now commits himself to encouraging sustainable living at the home for destitute children where he works and in the neighbouring villages, by installing compost and bio toilets, solar heating and cooking stoves, and recently experimenting with building a kiln to bake home-made water filters, as well as roof tiles.

• The young middle-class graduate staff of ISARA in Orissa, E. India, (several of them Brahmins) devote themselves to the untouchable and hill tribe peoples, living at their office, sleeping on the floor, washing under a cold water tap in the yard outside.

Each of these people has followed an inner imperative towards simplicity, for reasons of sustainability, solidarity, or simple practicality. For each the way of life is an integral part of the spiritual journey.

As for attachment, at a time when in the UK there is public debate about whether it should be legal to shoot a burglar, the following story is salutary. At a recent business meeting of the Religious Society of Friends in the West Country, the question of insurance came up, and the meeting was asked the categories under which risks might be considered. Suggestions were made of theft, travel, the building, personal liability and so on. Then a tall elegant elderly man stood up and said, "Can we put God on this list? I thought we were a religious society, not a financial one." Over lunch he told me that he and his wife never locked their doors. When their six children grew up they threw open their big empty house to homeless people – asylum seekers, ex-offenders, people on the street, and he recounted the richness of the networks that had formed, the postcards saying "Remember me? I came to stay with you last summer."

Among those trying to live a committed life, a lack of preoccupation with money is commonplace. Mike, remembering life as a warden of a Quaker Meeting House, says "there were no worries about a job or money. Every time I gave money away, I kept getting more!" Tax rebates, gifts – money kept coming in in the most perplexing way. Warren, who does not charge for his spiritual teaching work, lives from a trust fund, and says, "You get taken care of when you do this kind of work."

In a life devoted to God's purpose, the stripping down of possessions and habitat pares away the context of life: one is more purely an instrument of purpose. Do we need an identity created by status, a home, objects, a way of life that say in a shorthand understood by all: "This is me"? Reducing the clutter in our lives, whether in material objects, use of time or money, or in our religious practices, leads to a clarity of vision and a focus; a view of life and its priorities that is in itself simple. "The essence of simplicity is one-pointedness, an attitude and a life that is all of one piece, integrated and made one."

"The simplified man loves God with all his heart and mind and soul and strength and abides trustingly in that strength" (Kelly, 75).

13. CHASTITY

Lucinda and John married in their forties. Their work in the world is both separate and together. John, a former seminarian, works on spirituality in the business world; Lucinda leads pilgrimages in Italy and Soul Growth retreats and a three-year Living Spirit course in Canada. Both work on raising consciousness of the feminine in the world, sometimes raising hackles in the masculine world. When one is not able to be present for a commitment, the other stands in. Their life is centred round "monastic magnificence", which for them is contemplation brought actively into the world, doing the work of excellence for God. Increasingly they work towards a more monastic way of living.

Their day begins with narrative prayer together. They write their own prayers for others, finding quite miraculous the way their prayers are answered, and knowing that prayer is more powerful together: ("When two or three are gathered in my name...."). They then work from the bedrock of their prayer and the guidance that comes from it. Lucinda says that the fruit of not having children is the freedom to live like this: to be with God in a changing way.

Their marriage is a sacrament and, next to the Divine, the most important thing in their lives.

If God is relationship, how better to express the sacred than in relating to other human beings? Our struggles to live our faith in relationship reflect our fallibility, our insecurities, our lack of trust in each other, our inability to bring God into the relationship. Intimate sexual relationships bring special problems. Their intensity and connection to the primitive magnify the difficulties, as well as the joys. In the early stages in particular the tension between the glory of loving and being loved and a wish to control can interfere with the spiritual expression of union. The romantic ideal can lead to expecting too much of another human being.

Celibacy

So what about this third of the traditional monastic vows? Sex has long been a thorn in the side of the Church: the unruliness of this basic human instinct is not something institutional religion finds easy to cope with.

Celibacy is generally associated with monasticism, and correctly so in the case of Christianity. A Christian nun is "married" to Christ; complete faithfulness is to one master only: given to God. For Budddhists monasticism, a central way of life in most traditions, is governed by *vinaya* (a code of discipline) that requires celibacy. There are some exceptions: in Friends of the Western Buddhist Order there are no official monks or nuns, although some members do maintain celibacy. In Tibetan Buddhism a lama is a guru, not necessarily a monk. There are many married lamas; sometimes a man will spend many years in retreat before taking a consort, often on the instruction of his guru, then live in the monastery with his wife and children. The English Tibetan nun, Tenzin Palmo, said, "You don't have to be celibate, it's just for many people it's beneficial" (Mackenzie, 185). Gyan told me that his master has girlfriends. "Sex simply isn't an issue for the Tibetans," he said.

In Sufism too there has not in general been compulsory celibacy for those residing in a convent, and most Sufis are married. The eleventh-century compendium of teaching, *The Unveiling of the Veiled,* endorses the traditional attitude when it says: "No companionship is equal in reverence and security to marriage, when husband and wife are well suited to each other" (in Spencer, 318).

Ronald Rolheiser, himself a celibate Catholic priest, feels that too much has been made of celibacy as a spiritual ideal, and the celibacy of Roman Catholic priests is again in question and in the news. It was only in the tenth century that Catholic priests were asked to sign up to celibacy, not so much as a directive, but more a tidying up of what had become a difficult situation. The decision also has economic implications, as the Church is only expected to support one person, and not pay for a family and the education of children. The special dispensation given to a number of married Anglican priests who converted to Catholicism has given rise to an anomaly causing additional problems.

For many celibacy is a hard vow to keep and not always maintained – "a bit elastic", as one former monk described it. If the vow is not internalised but felt as an imposition, putting up with it will be the most positive response to be expected. And many are too young to understand fully what is being asked of them.

Philip Jebb, the headmaster of Downside and a Benedictine monk, writes frankly of his difficulties in the early days of his vocation.

Celibacy became much tougher, because I now had a much fuller appreciation of what I had "given up", especially at the level of companionship. I was very lonely. This was not the community's fault, either then or later; it was probably due to my extreme shyness, but it was real. I battled a lot with the mystery of virginity: how an apparently love-curtailing, life-denying call could really be the means to greater love...there could not be "answers". Christian virginity is not a problem to be solved but a mystery to be lived and is inseparable from the Easter mystery as a whole.

Boulding, 32-3

Another admits his "fear of sex" as a possible spur to the religious life. A nun of the same order writes of the pain of sudden realisation of what her vows meant:

On the day of my clothing...when the bridal theme was dominant, I felt a sudden upsurge of bitterness. I had freely accepted permanent sterility. I would always be barren. It took me long years to work through, to accept the fruitfulness of spirit which God offered me.

ibid., 107

On a recent TV programme in the UK a Benedictine monk said, "Sexual desires cease when the last nail is put in your coffin." A Catholic Dominican said that what he missed was not sleeping with someone, but waking up next to someone – not sex so much, but the intimacy of a relationship. A former Anglican monk told me that he had had an affair with another monk, but that they had been "reasonably chaste". A Catholic wrote that in the monastery underworld it was quite acceptable to be passionately committed to another.

The problems with celibacy in the Catholic Church have been very public: the sexual abuse of children by priests one symptom of a prevalent problem. Shockingly, three of the men I talked to had been sexually abused by priests – one as a child; one as a young man, leading to a profound mistrust of spiritual authority; and the third as a monk, leading to a mental breakdown and leaving his order.

So, what is the reason for sexual abstinence? One Benedictine monk viewed his self-denial now as being for the sake of something greater in the future. Mother Teresa famously said that all her energy was channelled sex. Another nun told me that it doesn't make sense to be wanting physical satisfactions: "The vow of chastity changes your heart – it gets bigger as you include more and more in your love." It is not just sex that is prohibited, but the intensity of "special relationships". The heart is then available to embrace not just special friends but all. So is it the case that celibates have more to offer God? Does sexual activity or a special relationship interfere with our service to God?

An emotional attachment is commonly viewed as a distraction. But a distraction from what? Is love – the very nature of God – to be expressed in detachment? The Brahma Kumaris view celibacy as an aspect of purity and make it obligatory for full-time male and female members, including married people. Of the people I have spoken to, only two lay people have voluntarily become celibate: one just for a period; the other, a member of Opus Dei, since becoming a member at the age of sixteen. I asked the first woman if it had made any difference. She said it was hard to tell as there was a lot else going on in her life, but she felt sex was an issue in the spiritual life. The life-long celibate said that she felt called to apostolic celibacy: that it made her more available to do her work in different places than it would if she were married. It was saying "yes" to God's love.

Chastity

For those in the world there is obviously no requirement to be celibate, although, as we have seen, some have felt called to refrain from sexual activity. "Chastity", however, is in general an accepted part of a religious life. What does this mean? The Buddha said that one who was not able to live a life of celibacy should not be "unchaste": that is, "break the purity of another man's wife". One man described chastity as being more emotionally available to others. Similarly, the Iona community defines it in terms of consideration for others: not necessarily sexual abstinence but "the chastity of sensitivity, perhaps of denying ourselves a freedom we might legitimately expect elsewhere, for the sake of others". Rolheiser describes chastity as reverence, respect and patience and also talks about sleeping alone being (like other kinds of self-denial) a form of solidarity with those who do not have a choice. Many faiths will confine sexual activity to within the bounds of marriage; the prohibition of contraception in the Catholic Church is because sex is viewed as admissable only for the propagation of children. Members of the congregation (lay members) of Hare Krishna are forbidden illicit sex, i.e. outside marriage. In a world in which sex is so much to the fore, it is interesting to see what those living a committed life in the world feel is right for them. One Quaker told me that, somewhat to his surprise, he had refused sex with his partner before marriage.

Committed relationships

Several of the people I interviewed are married, and I asked how living in a committed relationship affected their spiritual lives. Interestingly, one man admitted that he had always felt torn, that his spiritual vocation felt almost like being unfaithful to his wife. Another married man said that when he was young he struggled with the duality of his sexuality and his faith, but now felt that sex was part of the joy of life.

In general it was the groundedness and joy of married life that was expressed in response to my question. Giles said that

having a family and relationships may SEEM like a distraction but actually I think it is an essential ingredient: it keeps me ordinary, connected up with the business of the present moment, helps me to be less self-obsessed. Surely this is the whole point about the balance between prayer and action: action means not just making baskets or book-binding but dealing with one's children and with the bank balance: and looking for what in Zen is called the Essential world in all of this.

Certainly family life offers opportunities on a daily basis to put into practice our compassion and loving kindness, as well as non-violent ways of conflict resolution. The relationship of a parent towards a new-born baby is the most common expression of the unconditional love we are called upon to offer.

A Kabbalah teacher talked of his joy in his marriage and expressed his view that life is to be lived and enjoyed. He feels that the Gnostics went wrong in their view of physical creation as evil, and commented on the puritan streak in the English. An Anglican priest, now separated from his wife, talked of his lovers; others have partners who are a strong part of their spiritual life; some are immersed in family life. Most of the single men and women expressed the wish for a partner, although a twice-married grandmother expressed her relief at a life without such a complication.

Gay sexuality

For gay men and women the question is even harder, as in religious circles gay sexuality is generally viewed as unacceptable. For one man, sexuality had always been accompanied by feelings of guilt, especially when he fell in love with a Catholic monk in India. He was helped first by the love of a woman, then by a relaxed affair with another local man. It was, he said, redemption. In the middle of crossing a river, he heard: "You are much loved". It was the affirmation he had sought, and a reawakening of the totality of his life. Now he could see his spiritual life and sexuality as existing together.

Farley, suffering as a sensitive boy growing up in a tough Southern American home, made up for that unhappiness when he met his life partner over thirty years ago. As a Quaker, he is completely accepted as a gay man. Sarah, barred from her monastic vocation by her sexuality, has also found her home in the Religious Society of Friends, and has settled down with her bi-sexual partner and their children.

The joy of sex

Given the negative history of the church's relationship with sexuality, it was good to read the Catholic priest Ronald Rolheiser's joyous affirmations. "Sexuality", he says, "lies at the centre of the spiritual life...sexuality is an all-encompassing energy inside us. In one sense it is identifiable with the principle of life itself" (182/4). In describing this "sacred energy" he is at one with those within the Church and other religions who have asserted the importance of sex, and the importance of not devaluing it by promiscuity. In saying that it encompasses "love, communion, community, friendship, family, affection, wholeness, consummation, creativity, self-perpetuation, immortality, joy delight, humour and self-transcendence" (185), Rolheiser is certainly making big claims.

Charles Pickstone, a married Anglican priest, has also written on the subject. "Certainly," he says, "sex is sacramental: it opens up the deep structures of life and, rather than providing an escape, actually roots people in the present...Sex is where matter and mind, body and spirit, meet; sex is therefore the spirituality that reveals the sacramental richness of matter...sexuality at its best puts us in touch with reality" (238).

What about other religions? Judaism has had no such traditional hang-ups about sex: indeed Jews have been bidden to "go forth and multiply" as the large families of, for instance, Orthodox Jews, bear witness. Tantric traditions of Hinduism and Buddhism celebrate the deep spiritual value of the senses and the body. Sex and the body are sacramental and fundamental to incarnation.

This joyful acceptance of the place of sex in human life was echoed by many of the people I spoke to. Peter felt that "what we have lost, if we ever had it, is the sensuality of God": the sensuality expressed in the Song of Solomon, in the Sufi mystic poet, Rumi, and in much of medieval English mysticism. Sensuality directed toward God, and not dissipated towards others? Or a celebratory involvement of God in our relationships?

Certainly, when I had a partner who shared my faith, the experience was qualitatively different: our service was together, both in the relationship and in the outside world. God was present. If we are in the world, it seems perverse to deny one of the greatest riches of human existence.

Perhaps Rolheiser's summing-up is right. Christianity needs to learn more about sex; the world more about chastity.

14. INTERSPIRITUALITY

Where, then, is this eternal religion...to be found? It is to be found in every religion as its ground or source, but it is beyond all formulation. It is the reality behind all rites, the truth behind all dogmas, the justice behind all laws. But it is also to be found in the heart of every man. It is the law "written on their hearts". It is not known by sense or reason but by the experience of the soul in its depths.

Griffiths, 98

Interfaith

A respect for other religions and their discrete identities is an essential element of civilised life. We must, as the Bhagavad Gita says, honour our own life predicament; we cannot imitate another's. Interfaith is the word that describes the relationship between religions, and efforts to understand and to work with those of other faith traditions.

What lies at the heart of interfaith dialogue? Dialogue is in the end only the process of our own ongoing search for God. Leaving home, *fuga mundi* or relinquishing all certainties on our monastic journey, is exactly what we do in interfaith dialogue, for truth is essentially not a collection of doctrines but the living person of God in Christ. A measure of ... suspension of judgement is required in dialogue, particularly in the "seeing-judging-acting" process. We glimpse something of the other's faith and our judgement is temporarily suspended. Then we act, as it were, out of this suspension.

Moreover, rather than being on the look out for what might be of spiritual gain in other faiths, it is better to be open in a spirit of humility and poverty just as Christ emptied himself, ready to listen unconditionally to and welcome the other person. Men and women formed in a school of silence will be more open to the presence of the Divine Mystery and the simplicity of the Gospel, more ready for dialogue than someone equipped only with all the explanations and defences of Christian belief.

(Douai Abbey website, reporting on DIM-MID conference)

At a time when terrorism and the reaction to it threaten the harmony of multi-cultural communities, meetings of different faith groups are all the more important. After the 2005 London bombings, many churches made gestures of friendship to the Muslim communities in their midst, and within a few weeks one retreat centre actively worked to bring together all the Abramic faiths (Islam, Christianity and Judaism). In Toronto, Canada, the Pathways programme run by a United church is creating a multi-faith and healing centre to cater for the ethnic and religious diversity in its midst. In Israel, too, members of faith groups have shown the way in bringing together people from different communities.

It is important to recognise that different religious traditions meet the needs of different people at different times. Satish Kumar writes about the need for generosity and acceptance. "Whenever religious orders lose this quality, they become no more than mere sects protecting their vested interests."

A well-known novelist, talking on radio about her recent conversion to Catholicism, said that she felt that to consider all faiths equal was to undermine one's own faith. That is far from my experience. It might undermine one's *belief* if that belief were based on having found the exclusive truth. Religious belief, it is true, can lead to the taking of such exclusive positions, and to much of the conflict and violence that has been ascribed to "religion". I fail to see how it can be true of *faith*. You either trust a universal loving divine being or you do not.

Commonality of faith

At the level of belief and of religious observance and rituals, the differences between the major world faiths are not to be disputed. At the level of faith, the similarities of different approaches are striking, and at the mystic core the differences evaporate. It is at that level that most of the people in this book relate.

It is not a new concept: Happold's *Mysticism* is a collection of writings from all traditions and, seminally, Aldous Huxley's *The Perennial Philosophy*, the title of which recalls the name given to that common core. Thomas Matus, who has explored the connections between Christian Orthodoxy and yogic practice writes: "Whether we consider the light as 'God-consciousness' or as 'self-realisation', in reality it is one and the same...the awareness of being transformed into a new creature and the awareness of God's personal presence are one consciousness" (Matus, 94-5).

It is interesting that individual mystic traditions adopt that inclusivity when claiming that their tradition is universal. Although the Kabbalah and Sufism come, respectively, from the Judaic and Islamic traditions, both use the term more broadly. Sufis, in particular, "affirm that the organism known as Sufism has been the one stream of direct, evolutionary experience which has been the determining factor in all the great schools of mysticism" (Shah, 53), calling it "the yeast" in all religions.

The website of the Naqshbandi order claims:

The real sufi...is this universal human being, who has actually incarnated the very words of the Holy Book he reads – in this sense, he becomes the Koranic being for the Muslim, the Evangelic being for the Christian, the Hebraic being for the Jew, the Vedic being for the Hindu and the Buddha being for the Buddhist. He transcends the difference which divides and generates conflict and appreciates the difference which leads to unity, beauty and harmony, this difference which is a necessity for life.

Orthodox Muslims, however, regard Sufism as a part of Islam and the website is specifically Islamic and emphasises devotion to the *Shaikh*.

The roots of Quakerism are in Christianity, but it has always tried to be "open to new light, from whatever source it may come" (*Advices & Queries*, 7). Increasingly there has developed a "universalist" strand of Quakers who feel that that "new light" comes from the traditions of many faiths. Some have come from other faiths; indeed some still hold allegiance to another faith as well as membership of the Religious Society of Friends. (We have, for instance, two Muslim Quakers in our meeting.)

Gandhi, for whom interfaith reconciliation was a crucial part of his mission, was interested in the role of Quakerism in such a union. A friend of his proposed a founding of a *"religious fellowship which can be and will be joined by adherents of all the chief religions. I am not thinking of a syncretistic movement like Theosophy, which deliberately tries to take the best of each faith and joins them together. I am thinking of a union of hearts, a fellowship in which men of each faith, Hindu, Buddhist, Parsi, Jew, Muslim, Christian, all find themselves at one...And I wondered whether the Society of Friends, the 'Quakers' so called, could help to provide such a meeting ground."*

Gandhi's response was to ask if Quakers would be prepared to *"recognise that it is as natural for a Hindu to grow into a Friend as it is for a Christian to grow into one".* Many of us do. That is the whole point of the universalist position.

Kavanagh, 2004:142

Lucinda Vardey in her anthology of contemporary spiritual writings does not even give a label to the writers – as disparate as Sri Aurobindo, Jung, Thomas Merton and Matthew Fox – whose writings appear. When giving talks on mysticism I often read pieces from different traditions and challenge the audience to name the religions from which they come. Consider the following:

All help is given to you always, but you must learn to receive it in the silence of your heart and not through external means. It is in the silence of your heart that the Divine will speak to you and will guide you and will lead you to your goal. But for that you must have full faith in the Divine Grace and Love.

We cannot know God by talking or hearing others talk about Him; we can only know Him by plunging into the depths of our own being and entering that innermost region: the region that is silence.

Words stand between silence and silence: between the silence of things and the silence of our own being. Between the silence of the world and the silence of God. When we have really met and known the world in silence, words do not separate us from the world nor from other men, nor from God, nor from ourselves, because we no longer trust entirely in language to contain reality.

These pieces from different traditions are by, respectively, The Mother, Omraam Mikhael Aivanhov, and Thomas Merton (Vardey, 393 and 407).

My interest in mysticism and the commonality of faiths is perhaps not surprising. My mother, a Russian Jew, became a Kabbalist in her fiftics, and my father converted from Anglicanism to the Catholic church when I was five. Later in life he was much drawn to a monastic way of life, although he was never accepted into an order. His deep exploration and occasional practice of other religions was evidenced by the large folder of cuttings on all faiths that we found on his death. As I found my way to my own faith, I discovered to my surprise and delight that, despite our different labels, my father, my mother and I were in the same place.

Beyond religion

Abhishiktananda, the French monk who co-founded one of the first

Christian ashrams in India, Saccidananda Santivanam, in Tamil Nadu, spent much of his life building a bridge between Christianity and Hinduism. As his life became more and more contemplative, spending more and more time in his cave in the Himalayas, he became increasingly convinced of the merging of faith at the contemplative level. In his letters he explores the theology of the meeting of religions in depth: "It is only in a deepening of contemplative awareness in the Church that there lies any hope of the ecumenical and pan-ecumenical passing beyond that we need" (Stuart, 182). "Meditation on the Upanishads makes me more than ever keenly aware of the transformation through which the Church, and indeed all religions must pass. The age of religions...has passed" (*ibid.*, 274).

It is hard to overstate the radical nature of Abhishiktananda's position. He was writing at a time before the Second Vatican Council, a time at which even dialogue between faiths was not encouraged. His writings express an ability to go beyond the constraints of one faith, beyond labels, a coming together of East and West, of Christianity and Hinduism, that echoes in my soul, a confirmation of the commonality of all faiths. It is central too to the writings of his successor at Santivanam, Bede Griffiths, and the *sangha* (network) that bears his name "is committed to the search for truth at the heart of all religions". True to this purpose, in 2005 nine British members of the *sangha* were ordained as interfaith ministers.

Such an approach can lay itself open to the accusation of eclecticism, a "pick'n' mix" approach to religion, taking the best from each. This seems to me a shallow accusation, a misunderstanding of the profound truths of what Wayne Teasdale has termed "interspirituality" and defines as "the inclusive domain of the mystical...not an attempt to force synthesis" (175). Idries Shah, writing on the Sufis, calls it "the essential identity of the stream of transmission of inner knowledge" (370). To drink from the pool of human wisdom, to understand that there is one God with many approaches and that at the mystic core we are one – this seems to me part of the indivisible truth that we stretch for. "Religions meet where religions take their source."

Some of the people I interviewed have struggled with the narrow confines of a particular religion. Gwen was raised a Baptist, but her father encouraged her to explore other faiths. She taught at Sunday School, but then was sacked for bringing in material from other faiths. She is now with the Unity church which does not celebrate the Eucharist, includes some meditation in the service, and is more accepting of other traditions, including Native American. Within it, Gwen can follow her own path.

Increasingly, people are exploring the connections that can be made between people of different religions and those whose faith has found no community. Quaker Quest, an outreach programme that invites those attending to "share their spiritual paths", attracts dozens of seekers each week to its sessions all over the UK, and increasingly in other countries; the Seekers' Dialogue in Toronto began as an alternative to traditional Christian worship. Mary, as Minister of Congregational Development at a United Church in Toronto, Canada, wanted to offer an opportunity to people to seek a closer relationship with God without the trappings of traditional, organised worship. She was aware that there are many people who have been exposed to organised religion in the past and for a variety of reasons have chosen to stay outside religion. Many have pursued a path of personal spiritual discovery. With this in mind, Mary invited a number of her friends, from various faith (and non-faith) backgrounds to come together and look at what this new sacred gathering might look like. They discovered that each one had her unique perspective and through the process itself of discovering and sharing each other's visions, they created "community".

In his sixteen years as a spiritual teacher, Andrew Cohen's teachings have radically diverged from the traditional Eastern path that led to his own realisation, evolving into a comprehensive enlightenment teaching for the Western world at the beginning of the twenty-first century. While the essence of his message remains unchanging – pointing to the discovery of the Self beyond mind, beyond ego, beyond this world – his understanding and expression of what it means to live as that Self in this world continues to expand in breadth and subtlety. Most significantly, Andrew Cohen has redefined the goal and purpose of the spiritual path, in a vision that he calls Evolutionary Enlightenment. He shares these understandings in workshops in various parts of the world.

So what are the components of this commonality of faith? Wayne Teasdale considers that there are nine practical elements that make up what he calls "Integral spirituality":

1. Moral capacity
2. Solidarity with all sentient beings
3. Deep nonviolence
4. Spiritual practice
5. Mature self-knowledge
6. Humility

7. Simplicity of lifestyle
8. Selfless service and compassionate action
9. Prophetic voice and action

The Blessed Community

There is a particular connection between such people, those who, in the Quaker phrase, "know each other in that which is eternal". It can often be unspoken, a sharing through eye contact alone. There is a deep connection, sometimes during a meeting only of a few minutes. I remember sharing a cab with a black woman in Latin America. She asked me: "Have you heard the word of the Lord?" A few years before I would have been embarrassed, dismissed her as a born-again evangelical, and I am sure that our faith practices would be different. But on this occasion, answering literally, I said, "Yes, I have."

"Isn't it wonderful?"

"Yes," I said, and we looked deeply and joyfully into each other's eyes. Such encounters are intimations of eternity, a meeting of such profundity that time and place have no existence, and by them we are changed.

Thomas Kelly has written of this connection in his essay "The Blessed Community":

When we are drowned in the overwhelming seas of the love of God, we find ourselves in a new and particular relation to a few of our fellows. The relation is so surprising and so rich that we despair of finding a word glorious enough and weighty enough to name it…A new kind of life-sharing and of love has arisen of which we had only dim hints before…Some men and women whom we have never known before, or whom we have noticed only as a dim background for our more special friendships, suddenly loom large, step forward in our attention as men and women whom we now know to the depths. Our earlier conversations with these persons may have been few and brief, but now we know them, as it were, from within. For we discern that their lives are already down within that Centre which has found us. And we hunger for their fellowship, with a profound, insistent craving which will not be denied.

Kelly, 77-8

As he says, we do not create this community deliberately; we find it, and are amazed to find such depth of connection in near-strangers. It is grace, not our effort, that brings us to that place, and grace is no respecter of boundaries of geography or faith, of gender, education or of age. When we know God, we know God in each other, and that recognition can be in any of the chance encounters of our day. The first time I became aware of the power of that connection was in Bangladesh. On several occasions, when I met the eyes of a woman, there was an exchange of common humanity, motherhood, womanhood, that was beyond the language barrier, and intensely moving. That meeting of the eyes – "the windows of the soul" – is something which in the Anglo-Saxon culture is not common, a symptom of our fear of the other. In Madagascar a woman on a train told me she had been to England. Sensing a reserve, I asked if it had been a disappointment, if she had found people cold. Her answer was, "No one looks you in the eye, a whole day without looking someone in the eye, impossible."

By being aware of the eternal commonality in us all, we can

connect with people on the bus or in the shops; with a smile to those we pass in the street. As Kelly says,

> We, from our end of the relationship, can send out the Eternal Love in silent, searching hope, and meet each person with a background of eternal expectation and a silent, wordless prayer of love. For until the life of men in time is, in every relation, shot through with Eternity, the Blessed Community is not complete.
>
> *Kelly,* 88

The French make a distinction between *globalisation* and *mondialisation*: the latter a warmer, human whole-worldness. It is in this benign embrace that we partake of our essential commonality. A woman who lived in an ecumenical community for five years told me that "ecumenical comes from the Greek *oikoumene,* meaning 'the inhabited earth', 'the whole inhabited world': it's about **all** of us, the whole human race... **all** God's people, whether we name him or not."

As John O'Donohue says, "We are a family of the one presence" (303).

Karol: Canadian teacher, Thailand

Do you have a regular spiritual practice? *Yes, I have a regular living (spiritual) practice. On awakening, my day is offered to Love. During the day hours, I attempt to keep surrendering to the Love. In the evening I review the day, deal with unresolved issues, and sleep in the welcoming arms of Love.*

Do you have a spiritual director or "master?" *During my lifetime of nearly sixty years, I have followed this guru or that, this priest, or minister, or director, or that...always with the same outcome: I began to live THEIR wonderful way of spirituality, but not my own. I now am confident in the knowledge that I personally don't know much about anything spiritual and that my primary purpose is to allow Love to lead. This involves realising that I am not God, that I will not know the amazing life that I am given to live until I surrender my own desires to the One who is Love. It kind of means just "giving up" and letting Love have Love's way.*

Were you aware of spiritual leanings in your childhood? *I have never been able to separate spiritual life from physical life... meaning that my life has always been spiritual. This certainly does not mean that I have lived religiously those principles given me as a child. It does mean that I have lived spiritually in a physical world and come through it with bruises and bumps and distortions and handicaps BECAUSE OF whatever is within me.*

Did you ever consider becoming ordained or becoming a nun? *Yes, but only when my life became unruly and I needed something/one to reel me in. I am grateful that it was always a temporary leaning.*

How do you live your faith? *What is faith? Faith in what? A belief system? I guess the best answer is that I live my faith by surrendering myself to Love. The reduction of the "I" on a continual basis leads to this continual surrender.*

What is the balance of action and contemplation in your life? Are you happy with that? *Again, it's difficult for me to separate action and contemplation. Aren't we all, ultimately, spiritual beings, living a physical life? Isn't our ultimate call to live this mystery of Love within the society of humans? How does one separate action and contemplation? and why? Saint Francis of Assisi once said: "Preach the gospel at all times. If necessary, use words." What is the gospel? It is the Love.* To me, this quotation sums up my life – to live Love, to surrender to Love, to be harnessed and released by Love. Every action is wrapped in the Love. *Perhaps I'm trying to say that contemplation and action cannot be separated. Everything is united. Everything is done within the Love. On a grand scale, regard the Universe. On a small scale, regard your own hand...it is all one.*

How does your work express your faith; how do you bring faith to your work? *Again, what do you mean by faith? I am given to live my life in the only way I am given to live it....if that makes any sense. And by the way, the tremendous life that I am given to live has nothing to do with me and everything to do with Love. The greater the Love within me, the less I am apt to get in the way of It.*

Do you have an informal spiritual community? *Yes, it's quite informal, all right! Any community of persons living on the earth becomes my faith community. If I dare to define God, to define Love, by one set of principles, I rob Love of its mystery and reduce it to human terms. It is not easy to live without definitions, totally in the mystery, and that is perhaps why I have sometimes been tempted to "join" this group or that, to become a nun or lay minister, to feel secure in a title. Gratefully, I have not yet found it necessary to define me in these terms. I do appreciate people who live by one or another set of principles...ideas that help them to become all that they are. I learn from them but this just does not seem to be my calling.*

TAXING TASKS

Imagine the next person you dislike or disapprove of as a vulnerable child

Find a regular time of quiet with no external distraction

Observe a short time of silence before eating

Take your watch off

Spend a week without looking in a mirror

Sit in complete darkness, eyes open and feel your soul expand

Make up a rule for your own community (imagined or real)

Experiment with different forms of worship. Visit a synagogue, a mosque or a Quaker meeting

Consider volunteering through your local volunteer bureau

Pick up litter on your local streets for half an hour before breakfast

Find out if the chocolate you are buying has been produced in conditions of slavery

Walk barefoot in the park, aware of the grass between your toes

Wash the dishes, clean your teeth, in loving mindfulness

Try to bring yourself to a conscious centredness, increasing the frequency over a week

Say hello, have a conversation, with someone you usually ignore: the street cleaner, the parking lot attendant, a beggar

Try out a different form of spiritual practice

Think of four more tasks

FOLLOW-UP QUESTIONS

The following questions are suggestions for a personal journal exercise, or to consider in a study/reading group.

Chapter 1: Introduction

1. Were you aware of spiritual leanings as a child?
2. If so, did you tell anyone about them?
3. When and how did you first experience faith?

Chapter 2: A Life apart

1. Have you ever considered entering a monastery/convent?
2. If so, why did/didn't you?
3. Do you think that the monastic life has validity in the contemporary world?
4. What do you think the problems are?

Chapter 3: Out into the world

1. Have you ever considered being ordained?
2. If so why did/didn't you? And in what tradition?
3. What, if any, do you think is the place of the priesthood in the contemporary world?

Chapter 4: In the world

1. How do you relate to "the world"?
2. In what way are you "in the world"?
3. Do you belong to a religious tradition? If so, are you happy to be identified with it?
4. What aspects of being "in the world" are important to you?

Chapter 5: ...but not of it

1. What does being "not of the world" mean to you?
2. What aspects of modern life hinder your spiritual life?
3. What aspects of modern life do you opt out of?
4. Do others understand why you live as you do?

Chapter 6: Living in community

1. Have you ever lived in community?
2. If not, would you like to?
3. What do you feel is the appeal of living in a community?
4. And the disadvantages?
5. Do you have an informal spiritual community?

Chapter 7: Spiritual direction:

1. Do you have a spiritual director or "master"?
2. If so, how does the relationship work?
3. If not, do you feel you need one?
4. What do you think is the role of a spiritual director?

Chapter 8: Spiritual practice

1. Do you have a spiritual practice – as an individual? with others?
2. If so, what is it? And what effect does it have on your life?
3. If not, would you like to find one?
4. What, if any, do you feel is the value of a regular spiritual practice?

Chapter 9: Martha or Mary?

1. How do you live your faith?
2. What is the balance of action and contemplation in your life?

3. Are you happy with that balance?

Chapter 10: Faith in action

1. How does your work express your faith?
2. How do you bring faith to what you do in life?
3. How would you like that to change?
4. What can you do to bring about that change?
5. Have you ever been presented with work that is a challenge to your faith?

Chapter 11: Obedience: faithfulness

1. What are you obedient to in your spiritual life?
2. What does faithfulness mean to you?
3. Is the word "obedient" a problem for you?

Chapter 12: Poverty: simplicity

1. What do you feel are the most important reasons for leading a simple life?
2. What aspect of simplicity do you find most difficult?
3. If you were to try to live a more simple life, what would be your first step?
4. Do you believe in intentional poverty?

Chapter 13: Chastity

1. What place do you think sex has in the spiritual life?
2. Do you think that you have the right balance between individual relationships and your relationship with God?
3. Do you think celibacy is a good idea?

Chapter 14: Interspirituality

1. Do you feel you belong to a particular religious tradition?
2. Are you involved in interfaith dialogue?
3. What do you feel are the main barriers to understanding between faiths?
4. What do we have in common?
5. How can we share what we have in common?
6. What is your next step?

FURTHER READING

Abhishiktananda, *Guru and Disciple*, London: SPCK: 1974

Advices & Queries, London: The Yearly Meeting of the Religious Society of Friends (Quakers) in Britain, 1995

Anouilh, Jean, *Becket,* trans. Lucienne Hill, London: Methuen, 1963

Armstrong, Karen, *Through the Narrow Gate*, London: Macmillan, 1981

Barry, William A. and Connolly, William J., *The Practice of Spiritual Direction*, San Francisco: Harper Collins, 1986

Boulding, Maria (ed.), *A Touch of God*, London: SPCK, 1982

Burrows, Ruth, *Living in Mystery*, Lanham, MD: Sheed & Ward, 1996

Carretto, Carlos, *Letters from the Desert*, London: Darton, Longman and Todd, 1972

Chatterjee, Margaret, *Gandhi's religious thought*, London: Macmillan, 1983

Chittister, Joan, (ed.), *The Rule of St Benedict*, NY: Crossroad classics, 1992

Colegate, Isabel, *A Pelican in the Wilderness*, London: Harper Collins, 2002

Dale, Jonathan, (ed.), *Faith in Action*, London: Quaker Home Service, 2000

Dandelion, Pink, *The Liturgies of Quakerism*, Aldershot, UK: Ashgate Publishing Ltd, 2005

Dunne, Thomas, *The Reasons of the Heart*, London: SCM, 1978

Durback, Robert (ed.), *Seeds of Hope: A Henri Nouwen Reader*, London: Darton, Longman and Todd, 1998

221

Elgin, Duane, *Voluntary Simplicity*, NY: Morrow, 1998

Griffiths, Bede, *Return to the Center*, Illinois: Templegate, 1977

Hayman, Eric, *Fellowship in a Distracted world*, London: Friends Book Centre, 1934

Housden, Roger, *Retreat*, London: Thorsons, 1995

Huxley, Aldous, *The Perennial Philosophy*, London: Chatto & Windus, 1946

Jiyu-Kennett, Rev. Roshi P.T.N.H., *The Wild, White Goose*, California: Shasta Abbey, 2002

Kavanagh, Jennifer, *Call of the Bell Bird*, London: Quaker Books, 2004

Kelly, Thomas, *A Testament of Devotion*, NY: HarperCollins, 1992

Kornfield, Jack, *A Path with Heart*, London: Rider, 2002

Loring, Patricia, *Listening Spirituality*, vol. 1: personal spiritual practices among Friends, Washington DC: Openings Press, 1997

Mackenzie, Vicki, *Cave in the Snow*, London: Bloomsbury, 1998

Matus, Thomas, *Yoga and the Jesus Prayer Tradition,* Bangalore, India: Asian Trading Corp., 1992

Merton, Thomas, *The Asian Journal of Thomas Merton*, NY: New Directions, 1973

Contemplation in a World of Action, London: Unwin paperbacks, 1980

"Notes for a Philosophy of Solitude" in *The Power and Meaning of Love*, London: Sheldon, 1976

Spiritual Direction and Meditation & What is Contemplation?, Hertfordshire: Anthony Clarke, 1975

Nouwen, Henri J.M., *The Genesee Diary*, London: Darton, Longman and Todd, 1995

Seeds of Hope, London: Darton, Longman and Todd, 1989

O'Donohue, John, *Eternal Echoes*, NY: Bantam, 2000

Owen Jones, Peter, *Small Boat, Big Sea*, Oxford: Lion, 2000

Partington, Marian, *Salvaging the Sacred*, London: Quaker Books, 2004

Pickstone, Charles, *For Fear of the Angels*, London: Hodder, 1996

Pieris, Aloysius, s.j., *Mysticism of Service*, Tulana, Sri Lanka: Tulana Jubilee Publications, 2000

Prabhupada, His Divine Grace A.C. Bhaktivedanta Swami, *The Science of self-realisation,* London: The Bhaktivedanta Book Trust, 2003

Quaker Faith & Practice: The book of Christian discipline of the Yearly Meeting of the Religious Society of Friends (Quakers) in Britain, London: Britain Yearly Meeting, 2005

Rochelle, Jay C., "An Attender at the Altar", Wallingford PA: Pendle Hill, 1988

Rolheiser, Ronald, *Seeking Spirituality*, London: Hodder & Stoughton, 1998

Shah, Idries, *The Sufis*, London: Octagon Press, 1964

Sinetar, Marsha, *Ordinary People as Monks and Mystics*, NY: Paulist Press, 1986

Singh, Renuka (ed.), *The Path of the Buddha*, Delhi: Penguin, 2004

Steindl-Rast, David, *The Music of Silence*, Berkeley, Ca: Seastone, 1998

Stuart, James, *Swami Abhishiktananda: his life told through his letters*, Delhi: ISPCK, 1995

Suda, J.P., *Religions in India*, Delhi: Sterling, 1978

Teasdale, Wayne, *Monk in the World*, Novato, California: New World Library, 2002

Tolle, Eckhart, *The Power of Now,* London: Hodder &

223

Stoughton,1999

Traherne, Thomas, *Centuries,* London: The Faith Press, 1969

Vardey, Lucinda (ed.), *God in All Worlds*, NY: Vintage, 1966

Waddell, Helen, *The Desert Fathers*, London: Constable, 1936

Walshe, M.O'C. (trans. and ed), *Meister Eckhart Sermons and Treatises*, vol. 1, London: Element, 1979

Watts, Alan, *The Way of Zen*, Harmondsworth: Penguin, 1962

O

is a symbol of the world,
of oneness and unity. O Books
explores the many paths of wholeness
and spiritual understanding which
different traditions have developed down
the ages. It aims to bring this knowledge
in accessible form, to a general readership,
providing practical spirituality to today's seekers.

For the full list of over 200 titles covering:

- CHILDREN'S PRAYER, NOVELTY AND GIFT BOOKS
- CHILDREN'S CHRISTIAN AND SPIRITUALITY
- CHRISTMAS AND EASTER
- RELIGION/PHILOSOPHY
- SCHOOL TITLES
- ANGELS/CHANNELLING
- HEALING/MEDITATION
- SELF-HELP/RELATIONSHIPS
- ASTROLOGY/NUMEROLOGY
- SPIRITUAL ENQUIRY
- CHRISTIANITY, EVANGELICAL
  AND LIBERAL/RADICAL
- CURRENT AFFAIRS
- HISTORY/BIOGRAPHY
- INSPIRATIONAL/DEVOTIONAL
- WORLD RELIGIONS/INTERFAITH
- BIOGRAPHY AND FICTION
- BIBLE AND REFERENCE
- SCIENCE/PSYCHOLOGY

Please visit our website,
www.O-books.net

SOME RECENT O BOOKS

The Gay Disciple
Jesus' friend tells it his own way
John Henson

John offers the reflective reader a perspective on incidents and characters which at the very least make one think and which often help sharpen ones perception of what was, or might have been, going on. He manages to combine the strengths of the Sunday papers columnist approach with the radical evangelical message delivery of one who invites you to think! **Meic Phillips** ONE co-ordinator
184694001X 128pp **£9.99 $19.95**

The Laughing Jesus
Religious lies and Gnostic wisdom
Timothy Freke and Peter Gandy

The Laughing Jesus is a manifesto for Gnostic mysticism. Freke and Gandy's exposition of Gnostic enlightenment is lucid and accessible; their critique of Literalist religion is damningly severe.
Robert M. Price, Professor of scriptural studies, editor of The Journal of Higher Criticism
1905047819 272pp **£9.99**
UK and Commonwealth rights only

The Creative Christian
God and us; Partners in Creation
Adrian B. Smith

Enlivening and stimulating, the author presents a new approach to Jesus and the Kingdom he spoke of, in the context of the evolution of our Universe. He reveals its meaning for us of the 21st century. **Hans Schrenk**, Lecturer in Holy Scripture and Biblical Languages, Middlesex University.
1905047754 160pp **£11.99 $24.95**

The Gospel of Falling Down
Mark Townsend

This little book is tackling one of the biggest and deepest questions which, unexpectedly, brings us to the foundation of the Christian faith. Mark has discovered this through his own experience of falling down, or failure. **Bishop Stephen Verney**
1846940095 144pp **£9.99 $16.95**

I Still Haven't Found What I'm Looking For
Paul Walker

Traditional understandings of Christianity may not be credible perhaps they can still speak to us in a different way. Perhaps they point to something which we can still sense. Something we need in our lives. Something not just to make us decent, or responsible, but happy and fulfilled. Paul Walker, former Times preacher of the year, does not give answers, but rejoices in the search.
1905047762 144pp **£9.99 $16.95**

An Introduction to Radical Theology
The death and resurrection of God
Trevor Greenfield

This is a clearly written and scholarly introduction to radical theology that, at the same time, provides a contextualised and much needed survey of the movement. At times and in turns Greenfield is passionate, ironical, polemical and acerbic. An underlying wit surfaces in images that punctuate the text. This work is a significant and valuable addition to the literature available not only on theological writing but also cultural change. **Journal of Beliefs and Values**
1905047606 208pp **£12.99 $29.95**

Tomorrow's Christian
A new framework for Christian living
Adrian B. Smith

This is a vision of a radically new kind of Christianity. While many of the ideas here have been accepted by radical Christians and liberal theologians for some time, this presents them as an accessible, coherent package: a faith you can imagine living out with integrity in the real world. And even if you already see yourself as a "progressive Christian" or whatever label you choose to adopt, you'll find ideas in both books that challenge and surprise you. Highly recommended. **Movement**
1903816971 176pp **£9.99 $15.95**

Tomorrow's Faith
A new framework of Christian belief
Adrian B. Smith

2nd printing

This is the most significant book for Christian thinking so far this millennium. If this does not become a standard textbook for theological and ministerial education, then shame on the institutions! **Revd Dr Meic Phillips, Presbyterian**

1905047177 128pp **£9.99 $19.95**

The Trouble With God
Building the republic of heaven
David Boulton

Revised edition

A wonderful repository of religious understanding and a liberal theologian's delight. **Modern Believing**

1905047061 272pp **£11.99 $24.95**

A Heart for the World
The interfaith alternative
Marcus Braybrooke

This book is really needed. This is the blueprint. It has to be cherished. Faith in Jesus is not about creeds or homilies. It is a willingness to imitate Christ-as the Hindu guru Gandhi did so well. A must book to buy. **Peacelinks, IFOR**

1905047436 168pp **£12.99 $24.95**

Bringing God Back to Earth

John Hunt

Knowledgeable in theology, philosophy, science and history. Time and again it is remarkable how he brings the important issues into relation with one another ... thought provoking in almost every sentence, difficult to put down. **Faith and Freedom**

1903816815 320pp £9.99 $14.95

Christ Across the Ganges
Hindu responses to Jesus

Sandy Bharat

This is a fascinating and wide-ranging overview of a subject of great importance. It is a must for anyone interested in the history of religious traditions and in the interaction between faiths.
Marianne Rankin, Alister Hardy Society

1846940001 360pp £14.99 $29.95

Guide to Interfaith
Reflections from around the world

Sandy and Jael Bharat

For those who are new to interfaith this amazing book will give a wonderful picture of the variety and excitement of this journey of discovery. It tells us something about the world religions, about interfaith history and organizations, how to plan an interfaith meeting and much more - mostly through the words of practitioners. **Marcus Braybrooke**

1905047975 320pp 230/153mm £19.99 $34.95

The Hindu Christ
Jesus' message through Eastern eyes
John Martin Sahajananda

To the conventional theologian steeped in the Judaeo-Christian tradition, this book is challenging and may even be shocking at times. For mature Christians and thinkers from other faiths, it makes its contribution to an emerging Christian theology from the East that brings in a new perspective to Christian thought and vision. **Westminster Interfaith**
190504755X 128pp **£9.99 $19.95**

Back to the Truth
5,000 years of Advaita
Dennis Waite

A wonderful book. Encyclopedic in nature, and destined to become a classic. **James Braha**
Absolutely brilliant...an ease of writing with a water-tight argument outlining the great universal truths. This book will become a modern classic. A milestone in the history of Advaita. **Paula Marvelly**
1905047614 500pp **£19.95 $29.95**

Beyond Photography
Encounters with orbs, angels and mysterious light forms
Katie Hall and John Pickering

The authors invite you to join them on a fascinating quest; a voyage of discovery into the nature of a phenomenon, manifestations of which are shown as being historical and global as well as contemporary and intently personal.
At journey's end you may find yourself a believer, a doubter or

simply an intrigued wonderer ... Whatever the outcome, the process of journeying is likely prove provocative and stimulating and - as with the mysterious images fleetingly captured by the authors' cameras - inspiring and potentially enlightening. **Brian Sibley**, author and broadcaster.

1905047908 272pp 50 b/w photos +8pp colour insert **£12.99 $24.95**

Don't Get MAD Get Wise
Why no one ever makes you angry, ever!
Mike George

There is a journey we all need to make, from anger, to peace, to forgiveness. Anger always destroys, peace always restores, and forgiveness always heals. This explains the journey, the steps you can take to make it happen for you.

1905047827 160pp **£7.99 $14.95**

IF You Fall...
It's a new beginning
Karen Darke

Karen Darke's story is about the indomitability of spirit, from one of life's cruel vagaries of fortune to what is insight and inspiration. She has overcome the limitations of paralysis and discovered a life of challenge and adventure that many of us only dream about. It is all about the mind, the spirit and the desire that some of us find, but which all of us possess. **Joe Simpson**, mountaineer and author of *Touching the Void*

1905047886 240pp **£9.99 $19.95**

Love, Healing and Happiness
Spiritual wisdom for a post-secular era
Larry Culliford
This will become a classic book on spirituality. It is immensely practical and grounded. It mirrors the author's compassion and lays the foundation for a higher understanding of human suffering and hope.
Reinhard Kowalski, Consultant Clinical Psychologist
1905047916 304pp **£10.99 $19.95**

A Map to God
Awakening Spiritual Integrity
Susie Anthony
This describes an ancient hermetic pathway, representing a golden thread running through many traditions, which offers all we need to understand and do to actually become our best selves.
1846940443 260pp **£10.99 $21.95**

Punk Science
Inside the mind of God
Manjir Samanta-Laughton
Wow! Punk Science is an extraordinary journey from the microcosm of the atom to the macrocosm of the Universe and all stops in between. Manjir Samanta-Laughton's synthesis of cosmology and consciousness is sheer genius. It is elegant, simple and, as an added bonus, makes great reading. **Dr Bruce H. Lipton**, author of *The Biology of Belief*
1905047932 320pp £12.95 $22.95